An Expert's Guide to

CHESS STRATEGY

Fred Reinfeld

1976 EDITION

Published by
Melvin Powers
WILSHIRE BOOK COMPANY
12015 Sherman Road
No. Hollywood, California 91605
Telephone: (213) 875-1711

Published by arrangement with Doubleday & Company, Inc.

Printed by

HAL LEIGHTON PRINTING CO.
P.O. Box 1231
Beverly Hills, California 90213
Telephone: (213) 983-1105

Doubleday Paperback Books Edition, 1962

Copyright, © 1957, by Fred Reinfeld

Printed in the United States of America

ISBN 0-87980-221-9

CONTENTS

CHAPTER 1

CHESS IS FUN?

THE Spaniards have a memorable phrase for that terrible moment when the bullfighter takes his sword and prepares to kill his animal adversary which has become maddened with rage. It is the moment when he must kill or be gored—perhaps fatally. In the grand, stark Spanish phrase it is "the moment of truth."

All the toreador's skill and training and courage have to be concentrated into this one critical moment. He is either good enough to succeed, or he is an utter failure. There is no way to escape, no way to explain, no way to pretend. It is the ultimate test.

Every public performer has to face this test. I have often thought of it on the many occasions when I have heard Beethoven's great violin concerto played. The opening movement has a long orchestral introduction during which the soloist has nothing to do but stand and wait. It sounds easy, but it is probably the most difficult part of his ordeal.

He looks at the audience. He shifts his gaze from time to time. He plucks the strings to make sure they are in tune. He dries his perspiring fingers. He fidgets. He puts his violin in place, takes up the bow, and . . . nothing happens. For me this is a period of almost unbearable tension.

The toreador, the violinist, and the chess master, too, have the supreme moment of achievement when they must either

9

display their art at its greatest, or they fail miserably. In every field of human endeavor this same inexorable law holds true.

Even in chess? "After all, it's only a game!" Yes, even in chess—especially in chess. True, the master does not risk life and limb. But his livelihood, his reputation, and his prestige are at stake. Chess is peculiarly a field where they pay off only on winners.

Years of success and fame count for nothing in an individual game. A master may have a glorious record as long as your arm, but let him play one bad game and he may fail to win a tournament. Let him play one bad move in an otherwise flawless game, and that may be the move that costs him first place in the tournament!

Chess, to my way of thinking, is the greatest fighting game of them all. Every move is a test, every move of the opponent creates a new crisis.

There is no end to the tension. Meet one crisis and another one turns up. Solve one problem and a more difficult one appears. Unexpected countermoves, sly traps for the unwary, surprises that make your heart thump—such is chess even in its everyday aspects.

In such games as football and basketball the contestants get some release for their nervous tension in their physical exertions. Not so in chess, where the adversaries must sit and do all their fighting with their brains. This explains why many players fidget. Some wiggle their feet. Others, like the great Alekhine, twist a lock of hair unceasingly. Still others engage in nervous gestures which look comical to the uninitiated; but to the man who knows, all these gestures tell the revealing tale of unbearable tension.

It is this unremitting tension that explains the touchiness of the chess masters. Only people who are prepared to be incessantly combative can flourish in such an atmosphere. Nimzovich used to complain if his opponent got up from the table and leaned over a chair to scrutinize the position. Capablanca's opponents took it amiss when he grinned self-confidently as he fingered his red tie. (They objected to the red tie, too, for that matter.) Who knows, his grin may have been sheer nervousness.

Of course, players like you and me are lucky in this respect. When we do play a game, there is nothing world-shaking at stake. Unlike the masters, you are in the fortunate position of playing for the fun of it. Chess is only your hobby, not your livelihood.

But, as I have pointed out, chess is a great fighting game by its very nature. This is apt to make some people too tense. Perhaps they can't be philosophical about losing; perhaps victory means more than anything else to them.

In that case, they miss the relaxation they ought to be getting, and at the same time they lose sight of the fine points that chess has to offer. To such players I say, you can enjoy chess, and this book will show you how.

Again, there are players who lack self-confidence. These players, too, can learn from this book how to enjoy chess. For as they read they will be learning new skills, acquiring information that they can put to use in their own games. By studying the play of the winner, they can get an insight into winning plans and successful strategy. By studying the play of the loser, they can see how a player goes wrong, either by drifting or by unwittingly taking the wrong turn.

Such readers, having greatly improved their playing strength by reading and study, can then go back to playing with renewed strength, with greater self-confidence, with a clearer understanding of the struggle that forms the background of every game.

And there is something very encouraging about the games in this book. They are all played by masters, and much of the play is really magnificent. Yet some of it is marred by blunders, by lack of insight, by faulty decisions. And here you learn something that can be very gratifying:

Even the masters, you see, can go wrong on occasion! They are not infallible. Listen to a master after he has won a game, and he will bray that everything has gone off according to schedule. But don't be fooled: his exuberance is the true measure of his great relief. If the truth were known, the game was one long series of moments of despair, each time rectified by feverish searches for satisfactory resources. As I have explained, the tension of the struggle addles even the master's wits and temporarily turns him peevish and querulous. That is something to remember the next time you play a game of your own!

There are still other types of readers who can get a great deal of enjoyment out of this book. They may enjoy chess keenly, yet they may find themselves without any opponents. Or they may be working such exacting hours that they have no time for play. In that case, they can, through the medium of this book, find a number of delightful ways to continue their chess activity at their own convenience and in their own good time.

In fact, any player—anyone who knows the moves of chess—will find something here to whet his appetite for more chess, and to interest him in facets of the game that have previously escaped his attention. *Playing*, as such, is the most obvious way to enjoy the game, and everybody knows that. However, there *are* other ways to enjoy the game, and to many this will come as news.

One thing is certain: though you may want to acquire these chess hobbies for the sheer pleasure of it, you will increase your playing skill just the same. You will get a finer insight into the powers of the pieces; you will see how sensitively attack and defense are balanced; you will realize as never before that in chess a good plan is more precious than rubies.

In writing on this theme I speak from personal experience. In earlier times, when I had few responsibilities, I took keen pleasure in tournament and match chess. As time went on, my opportunities for serious play dwindled, until at last it became an impossibility for me. Yet this period has been one in which my enjoyment of chess has been richer, more satisfying than ever before. I believe that if I explain the circumstances under which this has come about, the reader may be able to profit as well.

Long ago I found that my irregular working schedules made it difficult to plan chess-playing sessions in advance. It began to be troublesome to enter a tournament which obligated me to play four hours at a certain time on a certain day of the week. (If the games were adjourned and had to be played off at another session, so much the worse for me.) Even offhand games were difficult to arrange. Sometimes I was available but my friends were not. Other times there were social engagements, family occasions, or other hobbies to be considered. Traveling can become a time-wasting nuisance, especially in the suburbs, and particularly in wintertime, when most of one's chess playing gets done.

So, without quite realizing it, I began to drift into a pattern which was radically different from my chess-playing routine of earlier times. *I began to rely on my own resources for chess diversion.*

As far back as my school days, I had always made a point of playing over the finest games of the great masters. Of course I enjoyed them enormously, but I am ashamed to say that in those days pleasure was a secondary consideration. I expected to set the chess world on fire; and so I studied these games eagerly, gulped them down by the hundreds in order to master the tricks of the trade, to become a fabulous technician, to become the master of a highly specialized skill.

Now my days of competitive chess are over—have been over for many years. But since then I have spent a great deal of time playing over the games of the great masters for my own pleasure. This involves no driving ambition, no nagging need to improve, no pangs of conscience for following my own sweet pace. I play over games when I please, discard them when I please, take them up again as I please. Relaxation is the keynote at all times.

To my way of thinking, these games are superb works of art. The sparkling combinations of Alekhine, the exquisite endgames of Rubinstein, the filigree technique of Capablanca, the bizarre surprises of Breyer, the startling originality of Nimzovich, the pure artistry of Morphy, the endless inventiveness of Anderssen —these and many more are all at my disposal.

Some games appeal to me so much that I play them over not once but many times, each time finding something new and highly enjoyable. In the hundreds of books in my chess library I have a treasure which will give me the keenest enjoyment for the rest of my life. Without stepping out of my house, I have right at my fingertips an inexhaustible store of the masterpieces of the masters. Many of these games, as I well know, were produced with hardship and suffering; but for me they represent pure pleasure. Some are recent discoveries; some, old friends; all of them delight.

I play over these games according to my mood. When I feel like delving into them deeply, I cover the moves with a post card and try to figure them out before uncovering the score to see what was actually played. I may not play over a game to the finish; after all, I am master of my own time and I can finish the game whenever I please.

On some occasions I am too tired or too busy to care to study a game very deeply. So I may merely pick up a book and glance over the diagrams of interesting positions, concentrating on the highlights and ignoring the rest.

In any case, I have found that it is always rewarding to examine the notes and alternative variations. This adds immensely to one's understanding and enjoyment of the games, especially when the annotator is a first-rate player and writer. The genial humor of Marco, the biting irony of Tarrasch, the entertainingly "different" views of Nimzovich, for example, give each game an added dimension of enjoyment. This comes through with entertaining piquancy when the annotator is a better player than the men who produced the game, or where he has a totally different point of view.

And while I am dealing with this facet of enjoying annotated games, I must point out that few players realize how much the annotator adds to their enjoyment. To put the matter on its simplest level: if you play over a game *without any notes,* you are likely to miss all or most of the fine points. You will be bewildered and frustrated; such a game will give you very little pleasure.

On the other hand, when you play over a game with notes, the picture changes. The more the notes tell you, the more you get out of the game. In fact, in that case "what might have been" becomes just as important, if not more important, than the actual play itself. The annotator shows you the mistakes; he points out the better moves that might have been played. He also enables you to appreciate the really fine moves, which might well seem pointless to you if you studied them on your own. And so you see that only a fine annotator can give you the game in all its beauty and all its meaning.

Of course, you are not tied to any hard and fast procedure. If you don't care to study the notes in all their detail, you can at least pick out the most essential items; no matter how you proceed you're bound to benefit. And here is something to think about: when you play your own games, there is a harsh, bitter finality about them. When they're over, they're over, and nothing can change the result. But when you're playing over games, it's fascinating to wander off on hypothetical byways and explore possibilities that never happened. It's rewarding to consider the interplay of two struggling personalities. It's thrilling to observe the ups and downs as first one player and then the other gets the upper hand.

When *you* play a game, it's often a tragedy of errors. When the other fellow plays a game, it's a comedy of errors. You experience no tension, no disappointment, no rage over an obvious blunder. When you play over a game, the thrills merely add to your pleasure. As a spectator, you have all the fun and none of the heartache.

And then there is this point to be considered. Sometimes the very intensity of our efforts defeats our purpose. I often feel that it's easier to learn when we are less tense about the outcome. I would therefore venture to say that when you play over master games for pure pleasure, *you're more likely to learn, and learn well.* In other words, whether you want to improve or not, you *will* improve your playing skill by studying master games for pure enjoyment. The absence of strain will help you. In this connection I often think of a tug of war, in which both sides are putting forth their most intense efforts. Suppose one side were to let go of the rope—what would happen? Why, their opponents would fall flat on their backs.

One of the troubles with chess study has been, you see, that we go at it with too much anxiety, too much worry, too much joylessness. All the fun disappears, and what is chess for if not to give us enjoyment? The strange paradox is, then, that if we do our chess studying for fun we are more likely to improve after all! Trying too hard may actually be a hindrance and a drag on our hope of improving.

There are, to be sure, other ways of enjoying chess. I must confess that when my attention was exclusively riveted on the practical problems of competitive play, I more or less ignored these areas of enjoyment. That was my loss—one that I deeply regret now.

In those days, for example, I rarely dabbled in composed endings, for they had no utilitarian value. These, by the way, are a kind of chess puzzle. The composer offers you a position in which he says that if one side moves first, a certain result can be achieved.

Such positions appeal to our curiosity, because at first sight it seems altogether out of the question to solve the puzzle. These endings are therefore delightful brain-teasers; they have the same appeal as detective stories or crossword puzzles or in fact any kind of puzzle. They challenge our ingenuity, and they goad us to considerable effort.

You can approach them in one of two ways. For example, you can resolutely put away the solution and work on the ending for hours, until you're ready to say, "Well, this darn thing simply can't be solved. Maybe the diagram is printed incorrectly; maybe the composer is crazy."

But you may be sure there's nothing wrong; *the solution is there.* When you finally give up and look at the solution, you will find that the basic idea was always right under your nose. In fact, you may have tried it and then discarded it because you missed the little gimmick that makes the solution work.

Few things in chess are as absorbing as these chess endings. The composers are particularly fond of using as few pieces as possible—every unit that appears on the board must have some functional value in the solution. These positions often look barren of possibilities, and in such cases the chess pieces are made to perform nimble gymnastics that are beyond the ken of most of us. The achievements that the composers are able to extract from the chess pieces verge on the unbelievable—but seeing is believing!

The enjoyment of chess endings is an acquired taste. The more you work with them, the more you will enjoy them. I am willing to claim that, page for page, a book of such endings offers perhaps the most rewarding pleasure that we can get from any aspect of chess.

But you can approach these endings in a different way. Maybe you don't care to match wits with the composer. Maybe you don't care to struggle for the solution. Perhaps sheer relaxation—idle, wayward, effortless—is your goal. In that case, you can simply set up the position and go directly to the solution. You will still get a great deal of pleasure in seeing how the solution works, how each unit plays its foreordained role, and how the seemingly impossible becomes quite feasible.

To introduce you to the delightful world of chess endings, I have started this book with a number of old favorites of mine which I first saw years ago and which still give me the same pleasure that I had the first time I looked at them. When I set up these positions I have the same feeling of thrilled anticipation that I get at the theater or at the circus when the performance is about to begin.

The world of chess problems is another of those enchanted worlds which have no practical value. They exist merely because they are beautiful, and because their beauty makes us happy.

In a chess problem the goal is simple: checkmate the Black King in a stated number of moves. The solution—there are myriads of tries but only one way of achieving the objective—works by force. If you start with the right move, you enforce checkmate no matter what moves are available to Black.

Here again there is a brain-teasing element that is very congenial to many of us. The construction of chess problems is based on interesting theories and techniques which are well worth studying. (Besides, if you are familiar with the theories and techniques, you can tell immediately from the layout of the pieces what the solution must be!) But even if you are unfamiliar with the techniques, you can still solve a chess problem by the old reliable blunderbuss method of trial-and-error. If you're willing to try every move on the board, you're bound to find the right solution eventually.

As a matter of fact, you can become a good rough-and-ready solver, with no knowledge of underlying theory, if you adopt the attitude of trying out the most *unlikely looking* first move. Composers, you see, avoid the obvious and shun powerful-looking moves. They favor moves that are unobtrusive, moves that on the face of it appear hopelessly ineffectual.

Many solvers never get further than two-move problems, which are made up of a White key move, a Black reply, and then the checkmate. Three-movers are much more difficult, but they're also much more fun. The extra move puts a premium on foresight, but it gives the composer a chance to clothe his ideas more subtly and use more refined strategy.

I think that when you delve into the section devoted to problems, you will be attracted by their brain-teasing qualities. And you'll find that three-movers are insidiously attractive, even if you find them difficult at first sight.

These, then—endings, problems, and games—are the three ways I offer you to enjoy chess. In this book I provide you with three keys to chess pleasure that I believe will give you lifelong happiness. Of all the chess books I have ever written, this is the one that was the most fun, because it has enabled me to share my chess pleasure with the reader. If through reading this book you learn how to enjoy chess, I shall feel most delightfully and handsomely rewarded. And if you become a better player—as I'm sure you will—that will be an added dividend of enjoyment for both of us.

CHAPTER 2

NEVER UNDERESTIMATE
THE POWER OF A QUEEN

Composed Chess Studies

NOT long ago I saw a chess study on which the composer had labored for twenty years. It was tricky, full of amazing details, thoroughly enjoyable—but think of someone working for twenty years on a composition that might give us a half hour's pleasure!

Of course the composer did not work every minute of the twenty years on the composition. He started off with an idea, or possibly the wisp of an idea. Then perhaps he put it aside for a while. But the idea nagged him, begged for completion. At odd moments he went back to the embryo composition; perhaps he gave it a complete format.

But there was some flaw—there usually is, at the beginning. So he put more work into it. He polished it, made the setting more pointed. It still wasn't right; that inarticulate but insistent conscience of the artist kept him at work. At last, years later, the composition was completed, and that first dim intuition was at last laboriously transformed into a work of art.

So much for the composer's working methods. But what does the chess study offer you and me?

At the heart of every chess study there is a paradox which I find very attractive. The chess study, like the sonnets of Shakespeare, the nocturnes of Chopin, or the exquisite coins of the ancient Greeks, is a miniature art form. It is tidy and neat, rigorous and flawless.

But don't let this tidiness fool you. Within the strict limits of the composed study you will find fireworks and a stylized brilliance rarely attained in over-the-board play. Here is excitement conjured up by a master composer in the quiet of his study. It is an art that unfolds serenely, far from the struggle and the excitement of tournament play. It is an art that will provide you with a lifetime of the keenest pleasure.

Chess studies are the riddles and whodunits of chess. All the evidence is provided for your inspection. The conditions of the solution are perfectly clear. Even the first move may be obvious. But from then on—be prepared for a jolt!

For in these studies you will find that the most delicate yet far-reaching fantasy achieves miraculous effects with a few pieces and Pawns. The impossible becomes feasible—but always with a deft little finesse that will leave you speechless with surprise and never fail to delight you.

Before we come to actual examples, let us be clear about just what a chess study is. You are given a position that might have arisen in an actual game—in fact, some studies have actually been inspired by real games. The material is greatly reduced; rarely will you come across a position that is cluttered up with a great many pieces.

White always moves first, and the condition is always stated: "White to play and win," or "White to play and draw." *The play is forced; that is, the intended result is achieved against Black's best resistance.* No matter how Black twists and turns, White must succeed—by one specific, foolproof line of play.

And of course it is just here that we find the great charm of the composed study. Black's play is often subtle and full of fine points; a suitable solution may seem impossible—and yet, it is there! It's up to you to find it.

Oftentimes when we examine one of these studies, the task seems altogether hopeless. But don't lose heart: remember that there is a foreseen solution, and remember that every unit on the board is there for some purpose. Sometimes, by reflecting on the presence of a measly Pawn at some particular square, you may hit on the solution.

There is another point to keep in mind. In many a game there are long dreary stretches where nothing of any great importance is happening. Not so in a chess study. Everything is to the point. The decision must be reached by violent moves—captures, checks, Pawn promotions, threats, all sorts of tactical motifs. Every move must tell, must have a forceful purpose. Indeed checkmate, the most violent move of all, is often the theme of the study.

From all this it follows that from the point of view of providing pleasure, the study is even more rewarding than a complete game.

The almighty Queen

The Queen, as you know, is the most powerful piece in chess. Consequently, you would expect that in composed studies the formidable power of the Queen is often shown to good advantage. And this is indeed the case. (*See Diagram 1*)

Believe it or not, White can either force checkmate or win the Black Queen! Given the reduced state of the material on the board, this seems impossible—yet it works.

As you will see, a series of elegant Queen moves by White will force Black's King into a checkmate position at the side of the board! White begins with:

Diagram 1

Study by H. Rinck

BLACK

WHITE

White to play and win

[handwritten: Qb1!]

1 Q-QN1! . . .

White threatens 2 Q-N5ch, K-Q5; 3 Q-Q5 mate. Black has only one move: *[handwritten: Qb5+, Kd4; Qd5++]*

       1 . . .   **K-Q5** *[handwritten: Kd4]*

Now surely Black is safe?

But White has an even more elegant follow-up:

       2 Q-N3!! *[handwritten: Qb3!!]* . . .

This threatens 3 Q-Q5 mate. *[handwritten: Kxe4   Qc2+]*

Note that Black dare not play 2 . . . KxP, for then 3 Q-B2ch or 3 Q-N1ch wins Black's Queen. So Black tries: *[handwritten: Qb1+]*

       2 . . .   **QxP ch** *[handwritten: Qxe4+]*

       3 K-Q6 *[handwritten: Kd6]* . . .

Suddenly Black finds that his Queen is in the way, for now White menaces 4 Q-QB3 mate. *[handwritten: Qc3++   Qf4]*

Black's Queen must move, yet such moves as 3 . . . Q-B5 will not do because of the reply 4 Q-Q5 mate. *[handwritten: Qd5++]*

True, Black can play 3 . . . Q-N7 or 3 . . . Q-R8, preventing *[handwritten: Qg2   Qh1]* the mate on Queen 5. But in that case White has 4 Q-QB3ch, ~Ke4~ K-K5; 5 Q-B6ch winning Black's Queen.   *Qc3+*

The only remaining possibility for Black is: *Qc6+*

     3 . . .   Q-R1   *Qa8*

Diagram 2

BLACK

WHITE

Now White has a forced win by a series of Queen checks:

     4 Q-K3ch *Qe3+* K-B5 *Kc4*

     5 Q-QB3ch *Qc3+* K-N4 *Kb5*

     Ka5 6 Q-QN3ch *Qb3+* K-R3 *Ka6 seeks protection of Black Q.*

If 6 . . . K-R4 White wins the Black Queen at once with 7 Q-QR3ch or 7 Q-R2ch. *Qa2+*

   Qa3+

     7 Q-R4ch *Qa4+* K-N2 *Kb7*

     8 Q-N5ch *Kb5+* K-R2 *Ka7*

Or 8 . . . K-B1; 9 Q-Q7ch, K-N1; 10 Q-QB7 mate. Note how far-reaching was the effect of White's third move.   *Kc8*   *Qd7+*   *Kb8*   *Qc7++*

     9 K-B7! and wins *Kc7*

White's threats of 10 Q-N6 mate or 10 Q-R5 mate or 10 Q-R4 mate are more than Black can stand.

Compare this position with that of Diagram 1. Remember that all the intervening play was forced!

In the next study, we again see how the power of the Queen prevails by means of "X-ray checks."* Yet there is an amusing "gimmick" here. *White wins Black's Queen, whereupon Black promotes another Queen, so that White's good work seems wasted. Now comes the best part of all . . .* but see for yourself:

Diagram 3

Study by J. Villeneuve-Esclapon

WHITE

White to play and win

Black has a far-advanced passed Pawn. If White is to win, it can only be by taking drastic measures. Such as:

        1 B-R6!   . . .

Threatening 2 Q-N7 mate. Black must capture the terrible Bishop.

        1 . . .   KxB

        2 Q-R8ch   . . .

The obvious move, which looks promising because Black's

---

* An X-ray check is one which attacks the King and another piece behind it on the same line. In this study, White's fourth and tenth moves are X-ray checks.

reply is forced. (When Black has only one move, we sense that we are on the right track.)

     2 . . .   K-N4
     3 Q-R4ch   . . .

Again forcing Black's reply. But now a great light begins to dawn: White is about to win Black's Queen by an X-ray check.

     3 . . .   K-B5
     4 Q-N3ch   K-N4
     5 QxQ   P-B8/Q

Diagram 4

BLACK

WHITE

All this clever preceding play of White's—was it just love's labor lost? No, says White, for by means of an ingenious "echo" theme he wins the new Black Queen as well.

     6 Q-K5ch   K-R3
     7 Q-R8ch   K-N4
     8 Q-R4ch   K-B5
     9 Q-B6ch   K-K6

All forced.

     10 Q-N5ch and wins

White wins the Black Queen!

Beautifully imaginative play—and yet, note how rigorously

the study is constructed. White's King has to be at King Rook 3 to guard the White Queen checking at King Rook 4 and King Knight 3. The White Pawn at King Knight 4 prevents Black's King from escaping to King Bishop 4 at moves 3 and 8. The White Pawn at Queen 3 prevents . . . K-K5 at moves 4 and 9.

Black's forces have been set down with malice aforethought too. Black's Queen at Queen Knight 1 and the new one at Queen Bishop 8 are placed just where White can win them by X-ray checks. Black's Pawn at King Knight 3 prevents . . . K-N3 at moves 3 and 8. Black's Pawn at Queen 2 prevents Black from guarding against 2 Q-N7 mate by playing . . . Q-N2 or . . . Q-B2 or . . . Q-R2. Black's Knight at Queen Bishop 1 makes it impossible for Black to guard against 2 Q-R8ch.

And so it goes. Every unit is placed just where it must be if the solution is to be worked out as planned.

Diagram 5

Study by K. A. L. Kubbel

BLACK

WHITE

White to play and win

In the above study White operates by a series of discovered checks and possible forking checks and X-ray checks to produce *a fantastic checkmate.* It seems unbelievable that such an arsenal of threats could arise from such a harmless-looking position.

White must start with a move that is forcing and leads inexorably to more forcing moves:

1 N-K3 dis ch! . . .

If now 1 ... K-R5; 2 Q-N4 mate. Or 1 ... K-R7; 2 Q-KB2ch, K-R3; 3 Q-N2ch leading to the same mate.

1 . . .	K-N6
2 Q-N4ch	K-B7
3 Q-KB4ch	. . .

And if now 3 ... K-N8; 4 Q-B1ch, K-R7; 5 Q-N2 mate.

| 3 . . . | K-K7 |
| 4 Q-B1ch! | K-Q7 |

Or 4 ... KxN; 5 Q-K1ch when White wins the Black Queen. White is driving Black's King to the Queen-side. Why?

| 5 Q-Q1ch | K-B6 |

(If Black did not have a Pawn at Queen Bishop 3, White could now win the Black Queen by N-Q5ch.)

| 6 Q-B2ch | . . . |

Again forcing Black's reply, for if 6 ... K-Q5; 7 N-B5ch wins Black's Queen.

| 6 . . . | K-N5 |
| 7 Q-QN2ch! | . . . |

An important point is that if now 7 ... K-R4; 8 N-B4ch, K-R3; 9 Q-N6 mate.

| 7 . . . | N-N6 |

By everyday standards, Black can be content. The annoying checks are at an end. Or are they? (*See Diagram 6*)

8 Q-R3ch!!   KxQ

If Black's King retreats, his Queen is lost.

9 N-B2 mate

Now how slyly White wove the mating net. Black's Knight and Queen Rook Pawn block off the Black King's escape.

Diagram 6

BLACK

WHITE

The almighty Queen?

From these enjoyable studies we can see that the Queen is capable of performing miracles. But there are some studies in which we see what is perhaps an even greater miracle—how weaker pieces harry and chivvy the mighty Queen.

What makes such studies especially entrancing is that they require very close co-operation on the part of the pieces opposed to the Queen. Such co-operation often results in beautiful tactical possibilities. Another remarkable feature is the wealth of detail and the ingenious richness of alternatives to the main variation.

These points are well illustrated in the following two charming studies.

In over-the-board chess we would expect Black to win because of his material advantage. Yet, as matters stand, White has a forced win! (*The mechanics of the winning process involve Rook moves which expose Black's Queen to capture by means of X-ray checks with the Bishop.*) Black's forces are as helpless as if they had been transfixed by a magician.

Diagram 7

Study by H. Rinck

BLACK

WHITE

White to play and win

1 R-R8!   . . .

It is obvious that Black loses after 1 . . . QxR; 2 B-B3ch (again the familiar motif of the X-ray check, which also operates in the case of 1 . . . Q-K3; 2 R-R6ch or 1 . . . Q-B5; 2 R-QB8ch).

Nor is 1 . . . Q-Q4 satisfactory, for then 2 B-B3 pins and wins the Black Queen.

Even 1 . . . Q-R2 will not do, for then comes 2 B-N6!, QxB; 3 R-R6ch.

So Black plays the only move left:

1 . . .   Q-R7
2 RxP!   . . .

Another possible X-ray check: if 2 . . . QxR; 3 B-K8ch wins the Black Queen. Beautiful play!

2 . . .   Q-N1

Forced. (*See Diagram 8*)

Diagram 8

   3 R-R8!   . . .

An echo theme. This time Black's Queen cannot escape to Queen Rook 7, as the Queen Rook Pawn has disappeared.

   3 . . .   Q-R2
   4 B-N6!   QxB
   5 R-R6ch and wins

At last White wins the Black Queen. An easy ending to solve, yet it is notable for its quiet elegance.

In Diagram 9 Black is considerably ahead in material, and ordinarily we should consider White's situation quite hopeless. Yet the caption says, "White to play and win."

Hint: Believe it or not, White's King Rook Pawn is the key to the win. Plenty of fireworks are about to shoot up into the sky, but it is the prosaic little Pawn that makes victory possible.

The winning idea is astounding: White gives a check with his Bishop, which can be captured *three* different ways!

   1 B-N5ch!!   . . .

The Bishop check attacks Black's King and Queen, and must therefore be captured. But how?

Diagram 9

Study by M. B. Newman

BLACK

WHITE

White to play and win

If 1 ... KxB then 2 N-Q6ch followed by 3 NxQ and White advances and queens his passed King Rook Pawn.

On the face of it, there is nothing wrong with the alternative 1 ... NxB?—yet this allows a quick checkmate after 2 N-B5ch. For example, 2 ... KxP; 3 N-B2 mate—or 2 ... K-R4; 3 N-B4 mate. This double mating method is very pretty.

1 ...   QxB

This gives White his hardest task. He wins the Black Queen, to be sure, but the win is still not clear.

2 N-B3ch   ...

If now 2 ... K-R4; 3 NxQ, KxN; 4 P-R6 and Black cannot stop the Pawn from queening. If 2 ... K-R4; 3 NxQ, NxN; 4 P-R6, N-Q3 White wins by the text method.

2 ...   KxP

3 NxQch   NxN

4 P-R6   N-Q3

Now White can advance 5 P-R7, but in that case Black has 5 ... N-B2 preventing the Pawn from queening.

Diagram 10

BLACK

WHITE

        5 N-B4ch!   . . .

The winning gimmick. Black's Knight cannot serve two masters.

        5 . . .   NxN
        6 P-R7 and wins

The Pawn queens after all. What a quiet finish after the thunder of White's first move!

The delayed sting

In some chess studies we can see the germ of a striking idea at first glance. But somehow or other the tantalizing jigsaw pattern does not quite fit together—generally because we miss some neat final finesse that puts all the details in proper place and proportion.

To find the delayed sting that is characteristic of such studies is not easy, because the process requires both a lively imagination and a sober eye for the precise. And yet if we fail, we are annoyed at ourselves for missing the "easy" solution. We are in the class of plodding Dr. Watson gazing in amiable stupefaction as his friend Holmes, on meeting a perfect stranger, notes that the man is left-handed, a veteran of the Boer War, and that he lacks one of his wisdom teeth, takes two lumps of sugar with his tea, and had an ulcer twenty-three years ago.

Now let's begin with a fairly simple example of the delayed sting and then proceed to more difficult studies.

Diagram 11

Study by A. Selesniev

BLACK

WHITE

White to play and win

White's Rook is attacked. If he plays some such move as 1 RxP, Black replies ... PxP dis ch with a dead drawn position.

We know as a general proposition that we need to start off with something more inspired than such a lackluster move. Suppose we begin with 1 R-B8ch, for after Black's reply (1 ... KxR), 2 P-N7ch (forking King and Rook) looks promising.

For the moment, you and I don't know what this will lead to. But in a chess study, a sequence of two forced moves is always promising. If two moves are forced, then maybe a third one will also be forced ... if only we can find the delayed sting.

So far we have:

1 R-B8ch!   KxR

The only move.

          2 P-N7ch   K-N1

Again the only move. And now what?

Diagram 12

BLACK

WHITE

This is the crucial position. If White hastily and mindlessly now plays 3 PxR/Qch, Black replies 3 . . . KxQ . . . and wins!

After all, Black's Rook is trapped; it cannot run away. *Why not look around for some other White move which may strengthen his position?* Obviously it cannot be a move of the White King, which would lose the mighty Queen Knight Pawn.

So, by a relentlessly logical process of elimination, we come to the only other possible move for White:

          3 P-Q5!   . . .

The delayed sting! Now Black can no longer protect himself against the queening threat. With a whole Rook ahead, he is completely helpless! He *must* play 3 . . . K-B2, allowing 4 PxR/B and wins.

Thus, after 3 P-Q5! Black is in *Zugzwang.* This ugly but useful German word, for which we have no convenient English equivalent, is applied to a position which has the three following characteristics:

1. A player—Black in this case—is menaced by one or more hostile threats.

2. As the position stands, the player has provided against every hostile threat.

3. Unfortunately, however, the player has to move, and when he does, he spoils his defensive dispositions.

All these three factors apply here, so we may say that after 3 P-Q5! Black is in *Zugzwang*, and must lose. This is one of the most fascinating concepts in chess, and one of the hardest for the ordinary player to grasp. It is easy to see that some brilliant blood-and-thunder move can reduce one's opponent to helplessness; but who would expect a mere Pawn move to have an equally crushing effect?

We see, then, that the right to move is not always an *asset*; sometimes, in rare cases, it may be a distinct *liability!*

Now we come to an ending which has an even more subtle delayed sting.

Diagram 13

Study by Rev. Saavedra

BLACK

WHITE

White to play and win

By ordinary standards White is lost, as he has only a Pawn for a Rook. But there is more involved here, for the Pawn is far advanced and just on the point of queening. Worse yet for Black, his Rook cannot retire to Queen 1 to stop the Pawn from queening.

All this is very encouraging, yet certain practical problems present themselves. White's King is in check. If he gets out of check the right way, he can win. If he gets out of check the wrong way, he will only draw—and in fact may even lose!

First, let's eliminate the wrong ways of moving the King.

If White plays 1 K-N7, then Black replies 1 ... R-Q2 pinning the White Pawn and preparing to draw by ... RxP. Strictly speaking, this is a kind of success for White—drawing in the face of such a great disparity in material. But it does not solve the stated condition of the problem: *White to play and win*.

Now back to Diagram 13. Suppose White plays 1 K-B5, attacking Black's Rook and relying on the fact that Black cannot retreat ... R-Q1. On the face of it, White wins at once.

Not so! On 1 K-B5 Black plays 1 ... R-Q8! Then if 2 P-B8/Q? Black has the X-ray check 2 ... R-QB8ch and wins. Consequently, after 1 K-B5, R-Q8! White must play 2 K-N6, whereupon 2 ... R-QB8 forces the draw.

This brings us to the winning method: *White will retreat his King to the second rank, when it will no longer be possible for Black to play ... R-QB8.*

Here, then, is the winning method:

1 K-N5!	...

Threatening to queen the Pawn. Black must keep checking.

1 ...	R-Q4ch
2 K-N4!	R-Q5ch

More of the same.

3 K-N3!	R-Q6ch
4 K-B2	...

Now it seems all over, for Black can play neither 4 ... R-Q1 nor 4 ... R-Q8. Thus the queening of the Pawn is assured.

4 ...   R-Q5!!

Diagram 14

BLACK

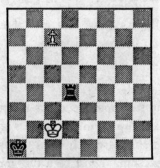

WHITE

Black is still fighting. If now 5 P-B8/Q?, there follows 6 ... R-QB5ch!!; 7 QxR and Black is stalemated!

And if White tries 5 K-B3 Black has 5 ... R-Q8! and again it seems that White is getting nowhere.

But White has a magnificent winning resource: *underpromotion.*

5 P-B8/R!!!   ...

At first sight this promotion to a Rook looks idiotic. Material is even, so what is there in this position to trouble Black?

But remember we said earlier that chess studies are concerned with *violent* moves and threats. Material is even, to be sure, but now White threatens R-QR8ch followed by mate next move.

Nor can Black save himself with 5 ... R-QB5ch??, for, thanks to White's underpromotion, the stalemate possibility has been removed.

Black has only one move to save him from immediate disaster.

5 . . .   R-QR5

Now at last Black has apparently saved the day, and all the fine points of the study have seemingly been exhausted.

But here again appearances are deceptive. For now comes the delayed sting, the finesse that justifies and ratifies everything that White has played so far:

6 K-N3!! and wins

White attacks Black's Rook and also threatens R-B1 mate. Black can put up no further resistance.

How impossible is "impossible"?

We have already seen many endings that seemed impossible of solution and yielded up a winning process after closer scrutiny. Yet there are some studies which seem to resist all our efforts. "Impossible!" we exclaim. "Must be a typographical error!"

Such studies are particularly satisfying when we finally see the solution. Great frustration is followed by equally great contentment. (*See Diagram 15*)

Here for example is a slick study in which the composer has cleverly masked his intentions. *In order to win, White must exploit his remaining Pawn to the utmost.*

The more we study this position, the more frustrated we get.

Black threatens . . . PxPdis ch, winning White's Rook. What can White do about it?

If 1 RxP, RxRch; 2 PxRch, KxP and the position is a draw.

If 1 P-N7 (hoping for 1 . . . KxR???; 2 PxR/Q), Black simply moves his Rook (say 1 . . . R-R1) and White cannot win as his Bishop is hemmed in and useless.

And of course if 1 R-N7ch, KxB; 2 RxP, RxRch; 3 PxR, K-N2 and Black draws.

What other possibilities remain? None. *Yet there is a win for White in this position.* One of the three White moves we have considered must win. Which one is it?

Diagram 15
Study by S. Kozlovski

BLACK

WHITE

White to play and win

Look at it this way. If White's Bishop were off the board, he would win easily: 1 P-N7!, R moves; 2 R-R8ch winning Black's Rook! And there we have it: White must get rid of his useless Bishop. Therefore:

| 1 R-N7ch!! | KxB |
| 2 R-R7ch | K-N1 |

Black's moves are forced—an indication that we're on the right track.

| 3 P-N7! | . . . |

If now 3 . . . KxR; 4 PxR/Q wins for White.

| 3 . . . | R moves |
| 4 R-R8ch and wins | |

The elimination of the Bishop makes all the difference. A difficult ending!

The situation in Diagram 16 seems even more hopeless. White can capture the Black Pawn to prevent it from queening, but in that case Black plays . . . BxN and draws. Or White can save his

Knight—but in that case Black queens his Pawn. Apparently there is no way out of this dilemma.

HINT: *White can win by forcing Black to capture the Knight with his King, leading to a position in which White has time to capture the Black Pawn and then win the Bishop by a pin or an X-ray check. This means that Black's King must be decoyed to his eighth rank or to the King Bishop file.*

Diagram 16

Study by N. Rossolimo

BLACK

WHITE

White to play and win

Admitting that we can see no way to proceed, let's look for forcing moves. All we can think of is a check—1 R-QB7ch or 1 R-N8ch.

Obviously 1 R-QB7ch serves no purpose, for after 1 ... K-Q1 Black still threatens to queen, White's Knight is still attacked, and White's Rook is insecurely dependent on the shaky protection of White's Knight.

What about the other check? After 1 R-N8ch Black has 1 ... K-Q2 or 1 ... K-N2. Let's examine them one at a time:

      1 R-N8ch   K-Q2

> 2 N-B5ch   . . .

This forces Black's hand—an encouraging sign. For if Black doesn't attack the Knight (say 2 . . . K-B2 or 2 . . . K-K2), White can simply play 3 KxP and wins, now that his Knight is salvaged.

But suppose Black does attack the Knight. If 2 . . . K-B3; 3 R-QB8ch again saving the Knight and making 4 KxP possible with an easy win.

This leaves Black with only one move:

> 2 . . .   K-Q3
> 3 N-K4ch   . . .

Black runs into the same dilemma. His King must attack the Knight, but 3 . . . K-K4 will not do because of 4 R-K8ch. So:

> 3 . . .   K-Q4
> 3 N-B6ch   K-K3

Now at last White can capture:

> 4 KxP!   KxN
> 5 R-KB8ch and wins

White wins the Bishop by an X-ray check.

Now let's return to Diagram 16 and follow the alternative winning method. Remember that Black's only chance is for his King to stick close to White's Knight.

> 1 R-N8ch   K-N2
> 2 N-B5ch   K-N3

Forced (why?).

> 3 N-R4ch   K-N4

Again forced (if 3 . . . K-R4; 4 R-QR8ch).

> 4 N-B3ch   K-N5
> 5 N-R2ch   K-N6
> 6 N-B1ch   K-N7

Now it seems that White has reached a dead end. The Black Pawn still threatens to queen; the White Knight is still attacked and has no more checks.

But White wins all the same!

Diagram 17

BLACK

WHITE

7 KxP!   KxN
8 R-N1 and wins

The pin wins Black's Bishop.

In each case White achieves the "impossible" with a series of forcing checks followed by a delayed sting.

The "impossible" draw

In over-the-board play we detest the drawn game as something drab and colorless. It is true that some drawn games are interesting, but when it comes to studies that call for a draw, they are all exciting. For each one poses a task which is seemingly impossible. And so the studies in which White is to play and draw are often the most difficult of all.

Take Diagram 18 as an example. At first sight, all is black despair. White seems thoroughly helpless against Black's queening threat, as 1 R-N1? is refuted by 1 . . . B-B8.

Yet White can draw by subtle moves that maneuver him into a stalemate position.

Do we have any forcing moves? Only one:

1 B-Q5ch!   . . .

Diagram 18
Study by J. Sehwers

BLACK

WHITE

White to play and draw

If now 1 ... KxB; 2 R-K3 stops the Pawn.

       1 . . .   K-Q5

Still preventing R-K3. White must try another check, but first he must interpolate R-N1 in order to entice Black's Bishop to King Bishop 8. Why this is necessary will become clear later on.

       2 R-N1!   B-B8
       3 R-N4ch!   . . .

Now Black must capture, else White can play 4 R-K4 stopping the Pawn from queening.

       3 . . .   KxB

But now it seems that White has only a few checks left, after which the Pawn will queen.

       4 R-N4!!   . . .

White's last move looks nonsensical, as Black's King Pawn can now queen. Yet there is method in his madness.

If Black plays 4 ... P-K8/Q, White has no moves and is stalemated!

Diagram 19

BLACK

WHITE

(*Note that White's King cannot go to Queen Rook 6 because Black's Bishop has been enticed to King Bishop 8. It is this factor that is an essential part of the stalemate.*)

If Black underpromotes to a Bishop, White's Rook is still pinned, so that again we have a stalemate.

If Black underpromotes to a Knight, White has 5 R-N1 winning a piece.

In any event, White is on the point of playing 5 R-N1, so Black must promote to something. Therefore:

4 . . .   P-K8/R

The last try. But White has a satisfactory answer.

5 R-N1!!   RxR

What else? But now White is stalemated after all!

But the classic drawing study of them all is this one, which seems as impossible as squaring the circle. (*See Diagram* 20)

How can White possibly draw? His King is behind Black's Pawn, so that any race between the two of them is sure to end in the Pawn's favor.

On the other hand, White's Pawn can be picked up at any time by the Black King.

Diagram 20
Study by R. Reti

WHITE

White to play and draw

Yet the composer, by an inspiration of genius, combines the weakness of White's King and the weakness of his Pawn into a powerful factor that forces the draw.

This sounds mysterious. Briefly put, the idea is this: *as White's King moves up to try to gobble the Black Pawn, it simultaneously approaches the point where it can protect its own Pawn and threaten to queen it.*

White begins with:

           1 K-N7   . . .

If now 1 ... K-N3; 2 K-B6! (threatening to capture Black's Pawn by K-N5), P-R5; 3 K-K5! (threatening to capture Black's Pawn by K-B4, etc.), P-R6; 4-K-Q6! and White draws! For example 4 ... P-R7; 5 P-B7, K-N2; 6 K-Q7, P-R8/Q; 7 P-B8/Qch. Just in the nick of time!

But suppose Black pushes on his Pawn at once:

           1 ...   P-R5
           2 K-B6!   . . .

Believe it or not, White can still draw in this apparently desperate position.

Diagram 21

BLACK

WHITE

If Black plays 2 . . . K-N3; 3 K-K5!, P-R6 (else White's King catches the Black Pawn); 4 K-Q6, P-R7; 5 P-B7 and White draws, as he can enforce the queening of his Pawn.

2 . . .   P-R6

Now 3 K-K5? loses: 3 . . . P-R7; 4 P-B7, K-N2; 5 K-Q6, K-B1! Black queens his Pawn, but White's Pawn is stopped.

3 K-K6!   . . .

Since White can no longer catch up to the Black Pawn, he makes sure of controlling the queening square of his own Pawn.

3 . . .   P-R7

4 P-B7 and draws

Black cannot prevent the White Pawn from queening: 4 . . . K-N2; 5 K-Q7, etc.

This study, with its almost geometric rigor, is the most difficult example we have encountered in the chapter. It is hard to follow, but it will well repay careful study. I can think of no better instance of the inexhaustibility of chess than this greatly simplified study which involves only four units.

To round out our appreciation of the beauty of chess studies, here is a quiz based on four more studies. Try to solve them yourself, and then check with the solutions on page 171.

QUIZ ON CHESS STUDIES

Diagram 22

Study by H. Rinck

BLACK

WHITE

White to play and win

White has several finesses to ensure the queening of his Rook Pawn.

Diagram 23

Study by F. Prokop

BLACK

WHITE

White to play and draw

White can play 1 QXP(N2)!! despite Black's discovered check!

Diagram 24

Study by A. Troitzky

BLACK

WHITE

White to play and win

How can White trap Black's Bishop?

Diagram 25

Study by D. Przepiorka

BLACK

WHITE

White to play and win

Which Rook move wins for White?

CHAPTER 3

LONG LIVE THE KING!

Chess Problems

EMANUEL LASKER, who was world champion for twenty-eight years, was very fond of chess problems. Many other masters have shared this taste for problems.

There are probably two reasons for their enjoyment. In the first place, many problem ideas and mating techniques have an inherent beauty that is irresistible to any lover of artistry in chess. Once you're bitten by the problem "bug," it never lets go of you.

But there is another element in problems that appeals to us. When we play a game with an opponent, we want to win. We also want to play beautiful, interesting chess. Sometimes these aims get into each other's way. We may win, but in the process we may produce a game on which our verdict is: "Putrid!"

On the other hand, we may play a beautiful game, and botch it at the very end. What chess player is not grieved by such an unfortunate outcome?

In the realm of problems this competitive angle is ruled out, and that is the way some of us prefer it. We are perfectly free to enjoy the beauty of chess without indulging in pernicious rivalry and petty spite.

Actually, however, there is an element of struggle in solving chess problems. This becomes clear when we consider the nature of problems. A problem has been composed with the requirement that a checkmate is to be fulfilled by White in a *specified* number of moves against any Black defense.

Thus, if the problem calls for a mate in *two* moves, that means that there is a first move by White which will result in checkmate on the next move no matter how Black plays. If you force mate in *three* moves, that does not solve the problem. You must fulfill the stated condition.

Secondly, there is only one solution—the solution predetermined by the composer. You can hit on many moves that *seem* to work, but more careful scrutiny will lead you to realize that only one "key move"—White's first move—will do the trick. (Once in a very great while it happens that a second satisfactory solution, not intended by the composer and overlooked by him, turns up. This is called a "cook." It is a serious artistic flaw and makes the problem valueless.)

And so, because the number of mating moves is strictly limited and because there is one and only one key move, the problem is a *challenge*. It is a challenge to your ability, to your ingenuity, to your determination. It has the elements of a puzzle, a riddle, or a mystery. It piques your curiosity and torments your imagination. It does not leave you at rest until you have the correct solution.

Terms and techniques

For the experienced problem solver and the problem composer, problem construction bristles with technical aspects that heighten his enjoyment of the subject. If these technical points interest you, you can follow them up in the bibliography at the end of this book. If you don't care to delve into these esoteric matters, you can still get a great deal of enjoyment out of problem-solving, just as many people enjoy listening to music without ever having played a note themselves or having studied theory, harmony, and counterpoint.

However, you will find that the introduction of a few fine

points in the following discussion will heighten your enjoyment of the problems. At no point will these technical explanations reach the point of becoming forbidding or boring!

To begin with, we can classify two-move problems on this basis: Is the key move one that threatens checkmate, or is the key move a pure waiting move that forces Black to commit suicide?

Let's begin with a problem that features *a key move threatening checkmate.* (By the way, though the first move may embody a threat, it will never—or hardly ever—be a check. A check or a capture for the opening move is frowned upon as being too obvious and too brutal, hence lacking in subtlety and artistry. In making your first tries toward solving, you can rule out checks and captures as likely key moves.)

Diagram 26

Problem by H. V. Tuxen

BLACK

WHITE

White to play and mate in two moves

The key move is *1-N-B3* threatening 2 N-Q2 mate. Black has eight possible moves of his Knight to stop this mate, as well as one try with each Rook; but White has a successful mating move for every try.

First let's examine the eight possible moves of Black's Knight. (A problem involving such a possibility is called a "Knight Wheel" problem.)

If Black plays 1 ... N-B7 (in order to answer 2 N-Q2ch with 2 ... K-Q5), he blocks off the defense by his Bishop. Consequently White can play 2 Q-Q3 mate.

If Black plays 1 ... N-N6 (in order to answer 2 N-Q2ch with 2 ... NxN or 2 ... K-Q5), he blocks off the defense of his Bishop by his Rook at Queen Knight 5. Consequently White can play 2 QxB mate.

If Black plays 1 ... N-N4 (in order to answer 2 N-Q2ch with 2 ... K-Q5), he blocks off the defense of his Queen by his Rook at Queen Knight 5. Consequently White can play 2 BxQ mate.

If Black plays 1 ... N-B3 (in order to answer 2 N-Q2ch with 2 ... K-Q5), he blocks off the defense of his Queen 4 square by his Queen. Consequently White can play 2 Q-Q5 mate.

If Black plays 1 ... N-K3 (in order to answer 2 N-Q2ch with 2 ... K-Q5), he blocks off the defense of his King 4 square by his Rook at King 1. Consequently White can play 2 R-K5 mate.

If Black plays 1 ... N-B4 (in order to answer 2 N-Q2ch with 2 ... K-Q5), he shuts off the square King Bishop 4 as a refuge for his King in the event of 2 R-N4ch. Consequently White can play 2 R-N4 mate.

If Black plays 1 ... NxN (in order to eliminate the threat of 2 N-Q2 mate), White replies 2 PxN mate.

If Black plays 1 ... NxP (in order to answer 2 N-Q2ch with 2 ... K-Q5), White replies 2 QxN mate.

If Black plays 1 ... R-N7 (in order to answer 2 N-Q2ch with 2 ... RxN), his Knight is unprotected. Consequently White can play 2 QxN mate.

If Black plays 1 ... R-K4 (in order to answer 2 N-Q2ch with 2 ... K-Q4), White replies 2 RxR mate.

On indifferent first moves by Black, White carries out his threat and plays 2 N-Q2 mate.

An even more refined example of *a key move with a threat* is shown in Diagram 27.

Diagram 27

Problem by N. M. Gibbins

BLACK

WHITE

White to play and mate in two moves

The situation is tantalizing. Black's King threatens to run away to King 4. What about a discovered check? If White tries 1 R-Q4 dis ch (despite the fact that checks are frowned on), Black has 1 ... RxB. If White tries 1 R-B2 dis ch, Black has 1 ... B-K4.

Correct is the pretty key move *1 N-N2.* The move is astonishing on the face of it, as the Knight can be captured three ways, including one with check. Yet the move works, and this is why.

We saw that Black has to have his Rook and Bishop free to defend against possible discovered checks by White. *The operating paths of Black's Rook and Bishop intersect at Black's Queen Knight 7 square.* Consequently the move of White's Knight throws Black's defensive dispositions into complete disorder.

If Black captures White's Knight with his Rook, he blocks the defensive function of his Bishop. If Black captures White's Knight with his Bishop, he blocks the defensive function of his Rook. And if Black captures White's Knight with his Rook Pawn, he blocks off the defensive function of his Rook *and* Bishop. This kind of mutual interference is known as the "Novotny theme," after a famous composer. Problem composers have achieved many lovely effects with it.

Let's examine the possibilities:

If Black plays 1 ... RxN, his Bishop is blocked, allowing White to reply 2 R-B2 mate.

If Black plays 1 ... BxN, his Rook is blocked, allowing White to reply 2 R-Q4 mate.

If Black plays 1 ... PxN dis ch, his Rook *and* Bishop are blocked, allowing White to reply 2 R-QR4 mate. (This effect, giving check by interposing to a hostile check, is particularly attractive.)

If Black plays 1 ... P-B5 (hoping for ... K-B4), White replies 2 RxP mate.

If Black plays 1 ... P-N5 (intending to answer discovered checks with ... P-N6), White replies 2 RxP mate.

If Black plays 1 ... K-B2 (hoping to get off the dangerous diagonal), White replies 2 R-B8 mate.

If Black plays 1 ... K-K4 (which gives him a defense to all discovered checks), White replies 2 N-B4 mate.

If Black plays 1 ... PxR, White replies 2 BxP mate.

"Waiters"

Problems whose key move is a waiting move are called "Waiting-move problems," or "Waiters." *In this type of problem the key move embodies no threat.* But Black is left in *Zugzwang* (see page 36 for an explanation of this term). *Whatever Black does, his reply permits some kind of mate on White's very next move.*

In Diagram 28, we have a lightweight but very pretty example.

Diagram 28

Problem by M. Euwe

BLACK

WHITE

White to play and mate in two moves

White's material advantage is overwhelming, but that's completely irrelevant in a problem. What matters is whether he can force checkmate in the stipulated number of moves. Such powerful-looking tries as 1 R-QN1 (threatening 2 R-N8 mate) or 1 R-QB1 (threatening 2 RxP mate or 2 QxP mate) are easily defeated by 1 ... P-Q3.

However, this problem is a "Waiter."

The key move is *1 Q-Q6*, offering the Queen and threatening nothing whatsoever. Yet Black is absolutely helpless!

If Black plays 1 ... PxQ, White replies 2 R-QB1 mate.

If Black plays 1 ... P-B3, White replies 2 Q-N8 mate.

If Black plays 1 ... P-B4, White replies 2 Q-N8 mate or 2 QxBP mate.

If Black plays 1 ... R-B1, White has a choice of 2 QxR mate or 2 QxQP mate.

On other Rook moves, White replies 2 QxQP mate.

The two "duals" (after 1 ... P-B4 or 1 ... R-B1) are artistic blemishes. Rigorous theorists favor settings with only one possible mating procedure.

Some Waiters have a situation in which each possible Black move can be answered by a mating reply on White's part. A full group of such "set mates" is called a "Complete Block."

When you look for the key move in such problems, however, you often run into a difficulty. Whichever move you choose is apt to spoil one of the set mates. Your task, then, is "to lose a move," so to speak. *Your key move must be one which leaves all the set mates intact, or which replaces the one or two that you may spoil.*

These points are nicely illustrated in Diagram 29.

Diagram 29

Problem by P. H. Williams

BLACK

WHITE

White to play and mate in two moves

Assume for a moment that it is Black's move in the position of Diagram 29. Careful inspection will show that any conceivable move by Black leads to immediate checkmate by White—for example if 1 ... QxBch the reply is 2 QxQ mate.

White's problem is that since he moves first, he must find a key move that does not disturb the checkmating possibilities.

The key move is *1 B-B7*. The set mates that remain intact are the following:

If Black plays 1 ... Q-Q3ch (or 1 ... Q-K4), White replies 2 BxQ mate.

If Black plays 1 ... R-N7, White replies 2 R/B2xR mate.

If Black moves the Rook anywhere else, White replies 2 R/B2-KN2 mate.

If Black plays 1 ... N-N1, White replies 2 QxN mate. (Bear in mind that Black's Queen is pinned by the White Bishop.)

If Black plays 1 ... N-B2 or 1 ... N-B4 (unpinning White's Knight), White replies 2 N-K4 mate. (Again, note that Black's Queen is pinned.)

If Black plays 1 ... N-N5, White plays 2 PxN mate.

One set mate has disappeared. To wit, if Black plays 1 ... QxB, White replies 2 P-B4 mate.

This is a very ingenious setting, with an interesting variety of mating possibilities.

We get a variation on this theme when *all the set mates are replaced by brand-new mates*. Problemists call this a "Changed Mate Block" or simply a "mutate."

In Diagram 30 we have a subtle and enjoyable example of a mutate.

As the position of Diagram 30 stands, Black is in *Zugzwang*. If he moves his Rook anywhere along the seventh rank, White replies N-N3 mate. Or if Black moves his Rook anywhere along the Knight file, White replies N/B1-Q2 mate. Finally, if Black shuts off a flight square for his King with ... P-Q6, White replies Q-K7 mate.

Diagram 30

Problem by C. Mansfield

BLACK

WHITE

White to play and mate in two moves

But when we seek a key move for White, we find that whatever he plays, he spoils the perfect position. Thus, if he plays
1 K-B7 or 1 K-Q8, he allows a Rook check. If he plays 1 R-B8
or 1 R-B6 he again allows a Rook check.

And if White plays a Queen move or a Knight move, he also
disrupts the mating patterns we have seen.

There is, however, *one* Queen move which sets up completely
new yet valid mating patterns. This is therefore the key move:
1 Q-R6. The problem is a Waiter, since White does not threaten
mate as the position stands. But Black is again in *Zugzwang*.

Thus, if Black plays his Rook along the seventh rank, White
replies 2 Q-KN6 mate.

If Black plays his Rook along the Knight file, White replies
2 Q-K2 mate.

If Black shuts off his King's access to the Queen 6 square by
1 ... P-Q6, White replies 2 Q-K6 mate.

The complete change of mating patterns is cleverly arranged
and makes a very pleasing impression.

In over-the-board play, a discovered check can be a fearful weapon. In problems, too, discovered checks play an important role in bringing the Black King to bay.

To give a discovered check we need two White units standing on a line with the Black King. The combination of these units is called a "battery." The unit that moves off the line to make the discovered check possible is called the "front man" or "firing man." The unit in back, which actually administers the check, is called the "rear man."

In some cases the firing man gives check as he moves off the line, thus producing a double check, the most powerful of all checks.

Sometimes a battery is deliberately created to give the Black King a flight square. No sooner does the Black King reach this deceptive refuge than the firing man moves out of the way, giving discovered checkmate! Such a battery—trained on the flight square—is called an "indirect battery."

This is nicely illustrated in the following gem, which uses only five units all told.

Diagram 31

Problem by S. Loyd

BLACK

WHITE

White to play and mate in two moves

At first this problem is puzzling. As the position stands, Black is stalemated. If White tries 1 K-Q4 or moves his Rook along the Queen Bishop file, the stalemate persists.

If White moves his Rook along the eighth rank, he allows Black's King to escape to the Queen Bishop file. If he moves his Knight, he allows Black's King to escape to King 2. No moves of the White Queen have any effect.

What then remains? A King move!

The key move is *1 K-B5*. This sets up a "royal battery," with White's King as the firing man and White's Queen as the rear man. (Temporarily White's battery is an indirect battery, trained on Black's Queen 2 square.)

If Black makes use of his new-found freedom by playing 1 ... K-Q2, White's battery operates decisively with 2 K-K5 dis ch— and checkmate!

If Black plays 1 ... KxN, White's Queen swings back for 2 Q-Q1 mate.

The effectiveness of the White Queen in two different directions creates a very pleasing effect.

Three-movers

Your true problem fan favors three-move problems because they give the composer a lot more scope for ingenuity and subtle strategy. For the beginning solver such problems may mean trouble because he cannot see too far ahead, and because he is unfamiliar with the technical devices involved.

The following three-movers are on the whole more entertaining than difficult. I have selected them with a view to bringing out some of the beautiful possibilities in this field. Each problem has some unexpected quirk that makes solving it a delightful task.

In Diagram 32 we have a situation, for example, that looks absolutely impossible to solve. And yet the "impossibility" is the key to the solution!

HINT: *Figure out the right way to promote White's passed Pawn.*

Diagram 32

Problem by V. Holst

BLACK

WHITE

White to play and mate in three moves

Black threatens to play . . . P-B7, stalemating himself. What can White do about it? Nothing, it appears, for if White promotes to a Queen or Bishop, the reply . . . P-B7 stalemates Black.

The position of White's Bishop is tantalizing. It seems to be involved in some mate threat, yet its own Bishop Pawn firmly blocks it. What to do?

The key move is *1 P-R8/N.* Here is the play:

      1 P-R8/N   P-B7

      2 N-N6   . . .

This releases the stalemate, as Black can—and must—capture.

      2 . . .   PxN

Suddenly White's Bishop is unleashed.

      3 P-B7 mate!

A delightful problem.

In Diagram 33 White is again faced with the problem of avoiding stalemate. The key move is startling because of its seeming irrelevance to the problem of forcing checkmate.

HINT: *The key move gives Black a chance to capture, thus relieving the stalemate.*

Diagram 33

Problem by C. S. Kipping

BLACK

WHITE

White to play and mate in three moves

The key move is *1 Q-QR1*, thus:

    1 Q-QR1   PxQ/Qch
Must.

    2 BxQ   . . .
But now the stalemate is lifted.

    2 . . .   P-N7
Again the only move, but now White can mate, because his Bishop has vacated the vital square King Bishop 6 for his Knight.

    3 N-B6 mate

In Diagram 34 we have another example of underpromotion

to prevent a stalemate. The small amount of mating force used creates a most artistic effect.

HINT: *If you promote the Pawn to a Queen or Rook, you cannot checkmate in three moves. So your problem is to decide whether to underpromote to a Knight or Bishop—and on which move! Remember, there is only one right way.*

Diagram 34

Problem by W. A. Shinkman

BLACK

WHITE

White to play and mate in three moves

The key move is *1 Q-R3*. This cuts down the range of White's King, but stalemate possibilities may crop up.

      1 Q-R3   K-N8

If White now plays 2 P-B8/Q? or 2 P-B8/R?, we find that Black is stalemated.

      2 P-B8/B!   . . .

This relieves the stalemate and at the same time makes checkmate possible next move.

      2 . . .   K-B7
      3 B-B5 mate

In Diagram 35 we sense that in some way White combines the threat of QxRP mate with attack on the Black Bishop. But it is not easy to see what the double threat is to achieve.

HINT: *Try all the Queen moves that attack the Bishop, and see what happens.*

Diagram 35

Problem by S. Loyd

BLACK

WHITE

White to play and mate in three moves

The key move is *1 Q-KB1*. There are five lines of play to be considered.

Variation A

            1 Q-KB1   P-R3

On 1 ... P-R4 or 1 ... B-N7 White mates the same way.

            2 Q-QN1   P-N3

Forced.

            3 QxB mate

Variation B

            1 Q-KB1   B-B6

On 1 ... B-Q5 White mates the same way.

        2 Q-Q3   P-N3
Again forced.

        3 QxB mate

Variation C
        1 Q-KB1   B-K4
On 1 ... B-B3 White mates the same way.

        2 Q-B5   P-N3
Still forced.

        3 QxB mate

The way the composer has provided for the same checkmate based on five different Bishop moves tells us that this problem is a masterpiece.

There are still other possibilities after I Q-KB1. If 1 ... P-N3; 2 QxB mates directly. An amusing alternative is 1 ... P-N6; 2 N-N6ch, PxN; 3 Q-R3 mate.

In Diagram 36 we have a situation that reminds us of the mating procedure in Diagram 31.

Diagram 36

Problem by H. A. Loveday (version)

BLACK

WHITE

White to play and mate in three moves

*White must find some way of relieving the stalemate danger.
He does this by forcing Black's King into a position subject to
scathing fire from a Bishop-Rook battery. This involves a paradox
—how can White mask the action of his Queen Bishop without
allowing Black's King to escape?*

This is known as the Indian theme.

Black threatens to stalemate himself by ... P-N5, as he will
then be left without moves.

White must succeed in lifting the stalemate position without
losing his checkmate in three moves. Here is how he does it:

1 B-QB1   P-N5

The stalemate position.

2 R-Q2   . . .

He blocks his Queen Bishop and thus relieves Black's stalemate position.

Note that White's Rook and Queen Bishop now form an
indirect battery aimed at Black's King Bishop 5, the only square
to which Black's King can move.

2 . . .   K-B5

3 R-Q4 mate

The double check is stalemate.

These, then, are the features of the Indian theme:

1. A White Queen, Rook, or Bishop moves along a line which
contains a *critical* square. (In this case, the critical square is
White's Queen 2, and the White move is 1 B-QB1, crossing
White's Queen 2.)

2. Black replies with a move that threatens stalemate (1 ...
P-N5).

3. White relieves the stalemate by moving a piece to the
critical square (2 R-Q2), which gives the Black King a move.
Note that White's second move sets up an indirect battery aimed
not at the square on which Black's King stands, but on the
square to which the Black must move. (In this case, that square

is Black's King Bishop 5. White's Rook is the firing man, White's Queen Bishop is the rear man.)

4. Black's King makes the only possible move, but this leaves him vulnerable to the action of White's battery. White's firing man moves (3 R-Q4 mate) giving a discovered or double check which forces checkmate at once.

Another very pretty theme is the Bristol theme, so called because it first appeared in the Bristol Tournament of 1861 in a problem by Frank Healey.

Diagram 37

Problem by F. Healey

BLACK

WHITE

White to play and mate in three moves

The point of the Bristol theme is that White clears a line for his Queen to enable her to give checkmate. The charm of this theme lies in the fact that the key move, which serves for clearance, looks absolutely nonsensical to the untrained eye.

In Diagram 37, you can at once appreciate the logical construction of the problem if you are told that *White's key move*

1 R-R1 *clears the first rank in order to enable White to play*
2 *Q-N1 and* 3 *Q-N1 mate!* This is how the solution unfolds:

1 R-R1   . . .

If Black now plays 1 . . . B-R3, White replies 2 Q-QB6 mate.
If Black plays 1 . . . B-B3, White replies 2 QxB mate.
If Black's Knight moves, White replies 2 Q-Q6 mate.

1 . . .   B-Q2

On 1 . . . B-K1 White proceeds in the same fashion.

2 Q-N1   . . .

Threatens 3 Q-N4 mate.

Black can stop this mate by playing 2 . . . B-N4, but in that
case he shuts off his King's only flight square in the event of
White's next move.

2 . . .   B-N4

3 Q-N1 mate

Note that Black's 2 . . . B-N4 makes it impossible for Black to
escape by means of 2 . . . K-N4.

All this is very pretty and extraordinarily ingenious.

These beautiful compositions have undoubtedly whetted your
appetite for a try at some problem-solving on your own. A chess-
problem quiz appears on the next page to enable you to try your
hand at solving. Solutions with explanations appear on page 175.

QUIZ ON CHESS PROBLEMS

Diagram 38	Diagram 39
Problem by O. Wurzburg	Problem by K. Howard
BLACK	**BLACK**

WHITE	**WHITE**

White to play and mate in two moves

White to play and mate in two moves

White starts with a King move!

White needs a key move threatening mate.

Diagram 40

Problem by J. Berger

BLACK

WHITE

*White to play and mate
in two moves*

Find a magnificent waiting move
with the White Queen.

Diagram 41

Problem by T. R. Dawson

BLACK

WHITE

*White to play and mate
in two moves*

Another example of the Novotny
theme (see Diagram 27).

CHAPTER 4

HOW TO ENJOY MASTER CHESS

How to Play Over a Master Game

BELIEVE it or not, there are chess masters who don't like chess. There are others whose favorite relaxation is ... bridge. Capablanca became a world champion even though he found chess boring and, later on, even distasteful. On the other hand, his successor, Alekhine, "lived for chess and chess alone."

I feel sorry for the man who doesn't play chess, for he is missing what I consider one of life's greatest pleasures. While there is much that chess has to offer, I think the most delectable chess enjoyment of all is the habit of playing over the games of the great chess masters.

Such a game is both a sporting contest and an outstanding work of art. Playing over a master game is like having a seat at the World Series; it is also comparable to looking at a painting by Rembrandt, or listening to an opera by Mozart, or seeing one of Shakespeare's masterpieces. A game of chess fashioned in the heat of battle by two great masters is one of the most enchanting of all works of art.

You may be surprised at the high value I attach to playing over master games. Perhaps you have even tried it and found it disappointing. In this field, as in many others, you have to know what you want and how you can achieve it.

You can play over games for enjoyment, or for instruction, or

73

a combination of both. Or you may merely play over games to "kill time"—to pass an odd quarter of an hour in an agreeable way. Depending on what you want out of the game, your approach must be different in each case.

If you want to play over a game fairly rapidly and nonchalantly, without concentrating on it, you will do best to play over a game without annotations. Or, if it has notes, ignore them. If you feel like playing over a game after a day of hard, tense work, you probably do not relish the idea of concentrating on the moves and reflecting on their power and artistry.

It's a good idea to pick games that suit your mood. Select those that are short and entertaining—games that abound in tactical play.

These brief, pointed games are also ideal if you're looking for instruction—only in that case you'll want to study the notes. They'll explain to you why the bad moves are bad, and they'll show why the exploitation of the mistakes has a crushing effect. Don't shrink from playing over a game a few times. After all, you wouldn't think of playing over a great symphony or concerto on your hi-fi phonograph once with the idea that you had grasped everything in that composition on the first hearing.

To get the maximum from any game you study, play it over once without notes just to get a first impression of it. Much of it will probably seem unclear. Then go over the game a second time, this time reading each note. If there are long, detailed notes, skim through them—all you want this time is the big picture. Then, on a third reading, you can at last fill in the details and get to appreciate the fine points of the play and the analysis.

Each of these three sessions will give you keen and growing pleasure. For few experiences are more gratifying to us than taking a game that at first seems a hopeless jumble and then creatively reconstructing the thoughts and struggles of the players until the game becomes for us a delightful work of art. Of course, the game is a work of art, whether we appreciate it or not. Only our attempt to understand it and enjoy it will make this game *a part of our own experience*.

Some readers have a habit of playing over a game on a big board and playing over variations in the notes on a small pocket set. This is a useful idea. They can move the pieces on the small board to their heart's content without disturbing the position on the big board. Nor do they get the position in such a mess that they have to go back to the opening position and replay all the intervening moves.

Incidentally, it would be a mistake to suppose that playing over games is a passive experience, on the order of looking at television. When you play over a game, you're an active participant. You try to figure out, or at least have an inkling of, what the players are getting at. "What would I do in this position?" must be your constant query, and, even though you will be wrong time and again, you will be mightily thrilled when your choice turns out to be the same as the master's. Above all, you will be an active participant in the game, and your interest in the notes will be sharpened; for they will often explain why the particular move you chose is not the best.

In playing over a game, it's a good idea to identify yourself with the winner and consider each move from his point of view. This will intensify your sense of appreciation, and if you can anticipate some of the winning moves, you will enjoy the play that much more keenly.

It's also a good idea to cover the next move in each situation with a card or piece of paper, so that you can really work out the move on your own. At first your moves will be wildly out of line; but, as time goes on, your batting average will keep improving.

In playing over games for pleasure, your procedure will be pretty much the same. In chess, it's rather pointless to separate pleasure from instruction. The more you learn, the more pleasure you will get out of playing over games. The more you enjoy them, the more effort you will apply to understanding the games.

This can be put negatively. If you don't get much fun out of playing over games, you're not likely to learn much from them. On the other hand, if you don't learn from them, you're not likely to get much pleasure from them. But you can approach these games with the safe confidence that a receptive mood will provide you with many richly satisfying experiences.

How to read and write

In every field, enjoyment comes only from some effort. In chess, many people deprive themselves of wide areas of enjoyment by failing to learn the chess notation. This is the system for recording moves made on the chessboard. The novels of Dickens and Tolstoy mean nothing to the man who is illiterate. Similarly, the whole glamorous world of master chess is lost to the man who cannot read chess notation. Consequently, if you are not familiar with chess notation, you will want to master it as quickly as possible. If you are already familiar with it, you will find it useful to review the following explanation in my *How to Be a Winner at Chess:*

"In order to be able to record moves, we have to give each square on the board a name.

"This is how we do it: each of the pieces in the opening position has a specific name. [Before going on with the explanation, set up all the pieces in the opening position.] The Bishop next to the King is called the King Bishop. The nearby Knight is the King Knight, and the Rook next to the Knight is called the King Rook.

"The pieces next to the Queen are the Queen Bishop, Queen Knight, Queen Rook.

"The horizontal row on which these pieces stand is called the *first* rank. Consequently, the square the King Bishop stands on is called King Bishop 1. The square the Queen stands on is Queen 1, etc.

"Each Pawn is named for the piece in back of it. Thus the Pawn in front of the King is called the King Pawn and stands at K2. If it moves ahead two squares, we write the move 'Pawn to King 4.'

"The vertical rows on the board are called 'files.' They are named for the pieces that stand on them at the beginning of the game. The file the King Rook stands on is the King Rook file. The first square is King Rook 1; the second square is King Rook 2, and so on, all the way down to King Rook 8.

"All these details are easy to grasp; but here is a point that troubles many players. White records his moves from his side of the board, while Black records *his* moves from *his* side of the board.

"Thus, the square that White calls King 4 is King 5 from Black's side of the board. White's Queen 2 square is Black's Queen 7 square. (Note that these numbers always add up to 9.)

"However, if you remember that you must reckon the names of the squares from the side that is making the move, you will have no trouble whatever with the chess notation."

In Diagram 42 we have a complete picture of the chessboard, with all the squares named for both sides. The first time you look at the keyed squares, they make up a confusing picture; but note how quickly the clear-cut pattern emerges.

The squares as named from the White side read from the bottom of the page going upwards. The squares as named from the Black side read from the top of the page reading downwards.

No reader, no matter how inexperienced, need have any trouble with chess notation if he is willing to devote a measly two hours to preliminary drill before playing over games. Think of it!—only two hours of determined study as the entrance fee to a lifetime of pleasure. Could the price be any cheaper?

Diagram 42

QR1 / QR8	QKt1 / QKt8	QB1 / QB8	Q1 / Q8	K1 / K8	KB1 / KB8	KKt1 / KKt8	KR1 / KR8
QR2 / QR7	QKt2 / QKt7	QB2 / QB7	Q2 / Q7	K2 / K7	KB2 / KB7	KKt2 / KKt7	KR2 / KR7
QR3 / QR6	QKt3 / QKt6	QB3 / QB6	Q3 / Q6	K3 / K6	KB3 / KB6	KKt3 / KKt6	KR3 / KR6
QR4 / QR5	QKt4 / QKt5	QB4 / QB5	Q4 / Q5	K4 / K5	KB4 / KB5	KKt4 / KKt5	KR4 / KR5
QR5 / QR4	QKt5 / QKt4	QB5 / QB4	Q5 / Q4	K5 / K4	KB5 / KB4	KKt5 / KKt4	KR5 / KR4
QR6 / QR3	QKt6 / QKt3	QB6 / QB3	Q6 / Q3	K6 / K3	KB6 / KB3	KKt6 / KKt3	KR6 / KR3
QR7 / QR2	QKt7 / QKt2	QB7 / QB2	Q7 / Q2	K7 / K2	KB7 / KB2	KKt7 / KKt2	KR7 / KR2
QR8 / QR1	QKt8 / QKt1	QB8 / QB1	Q8 / Q1	K8 / K1	KB8 / KB1	KKt8 / KKt1	KR8 / KR1

Here is what you do: select a game of about 35 moves in length. Play over the first five moves for each side, quite slowly and carefully. Read each move aloud before you actually play it.

Look back over the score, and make sure you have played each move accurately. Don't pay any attention to the underlying ideas and intentions of the players; disregard the notes; all you're interested in at this point is reproducing the moves.

Now go on and play another segment of five moves, and once more review what has been played. When you're satisfied that you've played the right moves, go on for another five. If any of the ensuing positions don't make sense; if impossible captures are indicated; if pieces are moved to squares already occupied by other pieces; if check is indicated in the score but no check is feasible on the position you've reached; then you know you've made a mistake in following the score.

Don't lose heart. Retrace your steps and find the mistake. Study it to see the principle behind it, and make a mental note not to repeat that *type* of mistake again.

Don't be discouraged. The first few tries may be troublesome, but the drudgery will be amply repaid later on, as playing over moves from a score becomes a matter of habit, without your devoting any conscious thought to it.

Pocket chess sets

Once you make up your mind to increase your chess pleasure enormously by mastering chess notation to play over master games, you'll find it useful to acquire a pocket chess set. The number of occasions for using such a handy set are really endless —for example, on a commuters' train, while waiting for an appointment, relaxing for a few moments during working hours, or studying an absorbing chess problem before going to sleep.

In addition, few of us realize how useful a pocket set can be when we're playing over a game on a big board with big pieces. As I've pointed out, the variations in notes are best played over and studied on a pocket set. In that way you avoid any disturbance of the actual game position on your big board.

Again, when you play over a game and make a mistake and reach an impasse, it's a good idea to leave the position intact and run up the intervening moves on a pocket set. Then you not only get the right position, but by comparing it with the wrong position you can see where you went wrong. This is a vital step in becoming an accurate reader of chess notation.

Some people complain that a pocket set gives them trouble: they cannot visualize the position on it. Habit and frequent use will correct these difficulties. But if you're adamant you can obtain a peg-in set. These are generally too large to be carried in a pocket, though they are small enough to be carried conveniently in a portfolio or luggage.

A peg-in set has small holes set into each square into which pegs at the bottom of each piece can be inserted. The pieces are miniature size but clearly molded. As far as I know, there is only one peg-in set on the market which is truly pocket size. Here are the dimensions:

board	4″
case	6⅝″ x 4¼″
King	⅝″

The whole set is made of plastic and the price is extremely reasonable.

What kind of chess set?

The selection of pieces and board is a very important one, because your playing pleasure will be dependent on them to a considerable degree. While there is no point in being extravagant, this is definitely a field in which shortsighted economy is out of place.

Here are some useful pointers:

In buying a chess set, make sure the pieces are *weighted and felted*. If the pieces are not loaded, they will tip over very often and cause confusion and irritation. If they are not felted at the bottom, they will scratch your board—something to bear in mind if you have an expensive wooden board.

Color is another important consideration. Most people prefer the standard black and white colors for their pieces. My own personal preference is for red and ivory, which are colorful and cheerful and always make me look forward with pleasant anticipation when I begin playing over a game.

The size of the pieces is another important consideration. When you get a set which is intended for playing with an opponent—you want large pieces—the King may be 4–5 inches high, with a board of proportionate size. For home use in playing over games, however, such a size is too unwieldy. My own set, which I have used with the greatest satisfaction for a good many years, has the following dimensions for the King: height, 3½ inches; base diameter, 1½ inches. This calls for a board with 2½-inch squares.

Most sets are still made of wood, but nowadays many are available in plastic. There are plastics and plastics. Even the "unbreakable" ones are not unbreakable. However, they are remarkably sturdy, and pieces may be dropped innumerable times without damage.

Naturally they may not be proof against systematic attempts at annihilation. If Junior uses your chess pieces for teething; if your dog likes to crunch them between his teeth; if your maid happens to brush some pieces off the board while tidying up your den; or if, in a fit of rage, you hurl a piece to the other end of the room—well, who can prophesy what may happen?

However, the burden is clearly on you to take loving care of your set and neatly store away the pieces at the end of every playing session. For most of us, our chess sets are among our most prized possessions and should receive the care they deserve.

Your board should be in harmony with the type and quality of your pieces. Never use a folding board, which is only false economy. All folding boards warp sooner or later, which is very irritating. In addition, they get hopelessly discolored by spilled liquids, which makes a disagreeable sight.

Wooden boards are handsome and lasting. The board I use has inlaid squares of birch and black walnut. Spilled liquid is readily wiped off without leaving a trace, and dusting is of course no problem. The board has a festive appearance which affects me psychologically; the combination of good-looking pieces and board always gives me a keen sense of anticipatory pleasure and heightens my enjoyment in playing over a game. These psychological factors are important, and it is sensible for us to cater to them.

A great game

And now at last the stage is set for that most enjoyable of chess experiences—playing over a very fine game produced by two masters at their best.

I have given a great deal of thought to this game, for by it my argument stands or falls. This is the game I have selected to convince you of the thrills and artistic beauties of master chess. It was played almost half a century ago in one of the great tournaments, but it still retains the freshness and charm it had on the day it was played. When we play over such a game, we realize with profound gratitude that it is the chess notation that keeps these masterpieces alive, long after the players who created them have passed on.

(The exciting ending of this game appears in my *How to Play Chess Like a Champion.* Readers who have seen the conclusion will be interested to see how the denouement came about.)

A quick bird's-eye view of the game will reveal its grand over-all trends.

In the opening stage (up to move 10) Black gets a lead in development because of inexact play by White.

As the middle game starts, White forces a weakness in Black's center Pawns with 11 P-B5! He is now set to exploit that weakness, but his provocative 14 P-B3 gives Black an opportunity to create exciting diversions.

Nevertheless White hammers away at the weak Pawns. Black courageously realizes that he must play with utmost energy to hold the position. By a series of splendid counterattacking moves beginning with 23 ... Q-R5! he establishes adequate counterthreats to hold the position.

However, at move 39 Black goes wrong and gives White the chance to win by a superb combination.

In all, a spotty but very thrilling game, with enough seesaws to delight us from beginning to end.

Carlsbad, 1911

RUY LOPEZ

WHITE	BLACK
O. Duras	*E. Cohn*
1 P-K4	P-K4
2 N-KB3	N-QB3
3 B-N5	. . .

Diagram 43 (*Black to move*)

BLACK: Cohn

WHITE: Duras

White's last move seems to carry a threat: 4 BxN followed by 5 NxP. At this moment it is only a sham threat, as Black proves by his reply.

3 . . .   P-QR3

Black realizes that in the event of 4 BxN, QPxB; 5 NxP, he can recover his Pawn effortlessly with 5 . . . Q-N4 or 5 . . . Q-Q5. Master chess is full of these unspoken dialogues and challenges.

4 B-R4   . . .

White does not exchange, as he prefers to maintain the pressure. Maybe his "threat" will become a real threat later on.

4 . . .   N-B3

Black develops his King Knight—a preliminary to castling. At the same time he counterattacks, menacing White's King Pawn.

If now 5 BxN, QPxB; 6 NxP, Q-Q5 and again Black recovers his Pawn handily.

5 P-Q3   . . .

White definitively protects his King Pawn. Now he really threatens 6 BxN followed by 7 NxP, winning a Pawn as his King Pawn is fully guarded.

Hence Black must take steps to protect his King Pawn.

5 . . .   P-Q3

Now Black's King Pawn is firmly guarded.

But notice this: Black's last move has considerably cut down the mobility of his King Bishop, which is hemmed in by his Pawn at Queen 3. Hence Black makes a mental note to try to improve the prospects of his King Bishop.

6 P-B4   . . .

A curious move. White restrains Black from playing . . . P-QN4, hurling back the annoying Bishop.

6 . . .   P-KN3

This is Black's solution to the problem of developing his King Bishop effectively. He anticipates White's P-Q4, which will open up the long diagonal leading from Black's King Rook 1. Once Black places his King Bishop on the long diagonal, this piece should have considerable scope.

7 P-Q4   . . .

A sudden change of front. White threatens P-Q5—a vicious attack on Black's pinned Queen Knight. (Thus White keeps up the pressure initiated by his 3 B-N5.)

7 . . .   PxP

8 NxP   . . .

Again White presses hard on Black's pinned Knight. (White's

Diagram 44 (*Black to move*)

BLACK: Cohn

WHITE: Duras

threat is of course 9 NxN, PxN; 10 BxPch winning the Exchange.)

What, you may ask, is White's plan? Presumably the masters, being the great players they are, foresee everything that is to come. The fact is, they don't. At this point they're still groping. Perhaps a bit later a glimmer of a plan may appear.

8 . . .   B-Q2

Black develops, in order to protect his pinned Knight.

Let's dwell for a moment on those words: Black *develops;* Black *protects.* Aren't they good answers to those perennial questions—" What do I do in the opening? How do I know where to play my pieces? How do I plan for the future? How do I avoid feckless drift?"

Wherever possible, we solve *short-range problems* in the opening. Black's pinned Knight was doubly attacked. Black realized this. Black parried the threat. Good!

In so doing, Black developed a new piece. Doubly good! In the opening, our watchword must always be, "Development and more development!" This limited but important goal helps us to play purposefully in the opening.

Now, what about White? He sees that Black is about to play (if allowed) 9 ... NxN; 10 BxBch (forced), QxB; 11 QxN, B-N2 and Black is tremendously ahead in development. (He would have three pieces out, to White's one.)

Mind you, White is well aware of the reason for his slight lag in development. It is due to his losing a move by playing 5 P-Q3 and 7 P-Q4.

9 NxN   . . .

White exchanges in a way more advantageous to him than the line shown in the previous note. No matter how Black replies, he will have doubled Pawns. Such Pawns can be weaknesses, as you will see later on.

So here we have the beginnings of a plan on White's part: he will try to exploit Black's doubled Pawns: How? Well, that remains to be seen.

9 . . .   PxN
10 Castles   . . .

White does not fear 10 ... NxP? for then the pin 11 R-K1 wins (11 ... P-KB4; 12 P-B3 etc.).

Meanwhile, as you will see on the next move, White is ready to take further action against the doubled Pawns. Black can forestall this with 10 ... P-B4, but in that case 11 B-KN5, B-N2; 12 N-B3 threatens 13 N-Q5 with a very annoying pin. (Note that in this variation N-Q5 becomes possible because Black advances ... P-B4. Black's doubled Pawns are unwieldy and awkward to handle. Thus we have a theme for the coming play. If the Pawns spell trouble for Black, he must make up for it by giving his pieces maximum mobility.)

10 . . .   B-N2
11 P-B5!

A nice move, nicely timed. Black can pick up a Pawn by the obvious 11 ... PxP, but the resulting tripled, isolated Pawn would be a serious weakness. Black's Pawn ahead would be purely academic, for his Pawn at Queen Bishop 4 could never be maintained.

Diagram 45 (*Black to move*)

BLACK: Cohn

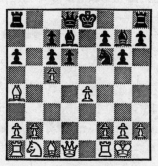

WHITE: Duras

As Black studies the position, he sees still another argument against 11 ... PxP. Suppose White replies vigorously with 12 P-K5 and Black plays 12 ... N-N5 (plausibly enough). Then comes 13 P-K6!! winning material, for if 13 ... BxKP; 14 BxPch —or 13 ... PxP; 14 QxN.

This is anything but inviting. Black hastens to castle—a safe and sound policy. Once he is castled, he genuinely threatens ... NxP.

11 ...   Castles

If now 12 PxP, Black has ... NxP, with excellent play for his pieces and a big lead in development. (With his King removed from the King file, he need not fear a pin on that file.)

12 N-B3   ...

White develops a new piece, and protects his King Pawn at the same time.

12 ...   Q-K2

Black likewise develops and protects his Queen Pawn.

13 PxP   PxP

Black still maintains his lead in development, and his Pawns are at last undoubled. But his Queen Bishop Pawn and Queen Pawn are weak, *because they cannot protect each other.* If Black plays thoughtlessly, White will build up lasting pressure, for example by means of B-B4 followed by Q-Q2 and QR-Q1.

Thus the policies are laid down for both sides.

14 P-B3   . . .

A provocative move! The right way was 14 R-K1!, preventing 14 . . . P-Q4 because of 15 PxP attacking the Black Queen.

14 . . .   P-Q4!

Finely played. The point is that White dare not win a Pawn by 15 PxP, PxP; 16 NxP? for after 16 . . . NxN; 17 QxN (or 17 BxB, QxB guarding the Knight), BxB he is a piece down. And if 15 PxP, PxP; 16 BxB, QxB Black's Pawn is amply protected.

Suddenly White's world seems turned upside down. Black's weak Pawns threaten to be transformed into a powerful passed Queen Pawn.

15 R-K1   . . .

White makes the best of it. The reply 15 . . . PxP; 16 NxP, NxN; 17 RxN would be feeble, as Black would be left with a backward Queen Bishop Pawn on the half-open Queen Bishop file.

But Black has an ingenious retort. (*See Diagram* 46)

15 . . .   P-Q5!

Sly play. If 16 QxP?, N-N5! attacking the Queen and winning, for example 17 Q-B4, Q-R5! threatening . . . QxPch as well as . . . QxRch.

If however 16 QxP?, N-N5!; 17 Q-Q1, Q-B4ch wins. If then 18 K-B1, Q-B7 mate. Or 18 K-R1, N-B7ch; 19 K-N1, N-R6 dbl ch!; 20 K-R1, Q-N8ch!; 21 RxQ, N-B7 mate!

16 N-K2   P-B4

Black has played cleverly, but now a new and difficult phase begins. Black's Queen Bishop Pawn is backward—that is, it is

Diagram 46 (*Black to move*)

BLACK: Cohn

WHITE: Duras

on a half-open file and cannot be protected by Pawns and must be guarded by pieces. White intends to attack this Pawn with all the power at his command and force Black into a disagreeable defensive formation. *Black must seek active counterplay.*

17 N-B4	B-K3

Even stronger was 17 ... B-N4!

18 P-QN3!	...

So that if Black carries out his contemplated 18 ... P-B5, he is left with an isolated and blockaded Queen Pawn after 19 PxP, BxP; 20 N-Q3.

18 . . .	KR-Q1
19 N-Q3!	...

Pressure on the Queen Bishop Pawn.

19 . . .	B-Q2
20 BxB	NxB
21 B-R3!	...

More pressure on the Queen Bishop Pawn—and a very annoying pin as well. White is gradually getting the upper hand after a slow start. The theme of the play is obvious: White attacks the Queen Bishop Pawn, Black defends it. *White has the initiative, Black is on the defensive.*

21 . . .   QR-B1

More defense for the weak Pawn.

22 QR-B1   . . .

Increasing the pressure still more—and he intends to pile it on by Q-Q2-R5, followed by doubling his Rooks on the Queen Bishop file. Little by little White is threatening to reduce his opponent to complete passivity.

22 . . .   B-B1

The Bishop leaves his proud diagonal in order to relieve the Black Queen of her degrading defensive task.

23 Q-Q2   . . .

The crucial position. White is dictating the course of the game, and if it continues along purely positional lines, White must inevitably win.

Diagram 47 (*Black to move*)

BLACK: Cohn

WHITE: Duras

If Black proceeds on exclusively defensive lines, he will double Rooks on the Queen Bishop file. For example: 23 ... R-B3; 24 Q-R5, KR-B1; 25 R-B2. Now, foreseeing that White is about to play KR-QB1, Black tries 25 ... Q-Q1, and there follows 26 QxQ, RxQ; 27 KR-QB1, KR-B1; 28 B-N2. (This threatens

BxP.) Black parries with 28 ... B-N2, and the play continues 29 N-N4!, R-N3; 30 N-Q5, R-K3; 31 R-B4. (Now the threat is 32 BxP!, BxBch; 33 RxB, PxR; 34 RxRch and wins. Black cannot play 31 ... R/K3-QB3? for then 32 N-K7ch wins the Exchange.) If now 31 ... R/B1-B3; 32 BxP!, BxBch; 33 RxB, PxR; 34 RxR, RxR; 35 N-K7ch followed by 36 NxR. White has won a Pawn and will soon win a second one.

This long variation is of crucial importance, and you must study it until you have mastered it thoroughly. Black may vary his play, but the moral is clear: if Black continues the policy of passive defense of his weak Queen Bishop Pawn, he will gradually be forced to the wall.

So Black must seek a diversion.

23 ...   Q-R5!

Just in the nick of time. If now 24 Q-R5, B-Q3!; 25 P-N3 (if 25 P-KR3, Q-N6), BxP; 26 PxB, QxPch; 27 K-B1 (or 27 K-R1, QxPch followed by 28 ... QxN), QxPch; 28 N-B2, N-K4! with the winning threats of ... N-Q6 or ... N-N5.

So White must drive Black's Queen away.

24 P-N3   Q-R4

Gaining time by attacking White's Bishop Pawn. In addition, Black holds in reserve an interesting finesse, based on the fact that White's Bishop is unprotected.

25 K-N2   P-B5!

Attacking White's Bishop. Hence White cannot capture the Pawn.

26 N-B4   Q-K4

27 BxB   P-B6!

The point. By interpolating an attack on White's Queen, Black saves his Pawn and establishes a formidable protected passed Pawn on the sixth rank. All this has been beautifully played by Black.

28 Q-Q3   NxB

White can now play 29 QxRP, but after 29 ... R-R1; 30 Q-K2

he is strictly on the defensive, and Black's connected passed Pawns remain a lasting menace. In the heat of the battle it is not pleasant to reconcile oneself to such passivity. White therefore creates a new crisis with:

29 N-Q5!   . . .

Diagram 48 (Black to move)

BLACK: Cohn

WHITE: Duras

White threatens 30 P-B4, and if 30 . . . Q-N2; 31 N-K7ch winning the Exchange. Or 30 P-B4, Q-Q3; 31 QxQP and wins.

Black finds the best reply to the threat.

29 . . .   RxN!

Black sacrifices the Exchange to remove the dangerous Knight.

30 PxR   QxQP
31 KR-Q1   . . .

Apparently decisive, as White threatens 31 QxQP and also 31 RxP!, RxR; 32 QxR as well as 31 QxRP.

31 . . .   N-K3!

Black cannot defend all the Pawns, but this move at least takes care of his powerful passed Pawns. For if now 32 RxP?, RxR; 33 QxR, PxQ; 34 RxQ, P-B7 and the Pawn must queen!

32 QxRP   R-R1
33 Q-K2   P-Q6!

Beginning a new critical phase. Black sacrifices the passed

Pawns in order to direct a withering fire against the White King. If now 34 QxP, RxPch; 35 K-R1, Q-KR4; 36 P-R4, N-Q5!; 37 R-B1, N-B4 with a tremendous attack.

34 RxQP ...

Diagram 49 (*Black to move*)

BLACK: Cohn

WHITE: Duras

34 ...   Q-KN4!

A seemingly overwhelming move with two brutal threats: 35 ... N-B5ch or 35 ... QxR. White finds the only way out, but it involves allowing Black to infiltrate into the seventh rank.

35 Q-K3!   RxPch
36 K-N1   Q-KR4

Threatens 37 ... QxRPch; 38 K-B1, Q-KN7ch followed by mate in two. Now that the days of Black's once-mighty passed Pawn are distinctly numbered, he has to make the most of his counterattack.

37 P-R4   Q-KB4

With the terrifying-looking threat of penetrating into White's game by ... Q-R6.

It seems at first sight that White should play 38 P-KN4 to drive back the Queen. However, after 38 ... Q-B5; 39 QxQ,

Diagram 50 (*White to move*)

BLACK: Cohn

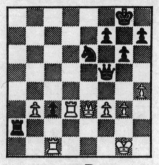

WHITE: Duras

NxQ; 40 R/Q3xP, N-K7ch; 41 K-BI, NxR/B8; 42 RxN, R-QN7!; 43 R-B8ch, K-N2; 44 R-QN8 Black is very likely to draw because of the powerful position of his Rook.

Note that 38 P-KN4, Q-B5; 39 R-Q8ch, K-N2; 40 QxPch??, K-R3 actually loses for White!

So White makes a very risky choice which is full of venom:

        38 R/Q3xP!   Q-R6
        39 R-B8ch   . . .

Diagram 51 (*Black to move*)

BLACK: Cohn

WHITE: Duras

Now Black should play 39 ... N-B1. Then, after 40 R/B8-B2 (White has nothing better), QxNPch; 41 K-B1, Q-R6ch and White cannot hope to win.

39 ...   K-N2?

But this loses. Too bad, after all that Black has been through!

40 Q-K5ch!   ...

A very important move. It protects White's King Knight Pawn, so that in the event of 40 ... K-R3 White can play 41 R/B8-B2 putting his King in perfect safety and assuring himself of eventual victory.

40 ...   P-B3

Now how is White to save his Queen and prevent ... Q-N7 mate?

Diagram 52 (White to move)

BLACK: Cohn

WHITE: Duras

Now White unfolds the first of a series of staggering surprise moves.

41 R/B1-B7ch!!. ...

If now 41 ... NxR; 42 RxNch, K-R3; 43 Q-B4ch, P-N4; 44 QxBPch, K-R4; 45 RxP mate or 45 QxP mate.

41 ...   K-R3

42 Q-K3ch   P-N4
43 PxPch   . . .

And if here 43 . . . K-N3; 44 R-KN8ch wins for White.

Diagram 53 (*Black to move*)

BLACK: Cohn

WHITE: Duras

Black can try 43 . . . PxP, hoping for 44 QxNch?!, QxQ; 45 R-B6, whereupon 45 . . . R-R8ch! forces a neat perpetual check.

But on 43 . . . PxP White plays 44 R-B2, QxNPch; 45 K-B1, Q-R6ch; 46 K-K2 and White's King escapes the checks by fleeing to the Queen-side, after which his passed Pawn should win for him.

43 . . .   NxP
44 RxPch!!   KxR

Now White has a magnificent win.

45 Q-K7ch   K-N3

Forced.

46 R-KN8ch   K-B4

Diagram 54 (*White to move*)

BLACK: Cohn

WHITE: Duras

47 RxNch!! ...

This is the end, for if 47 ... PxR; 48 Q-Q7ch wins Black's Queen.

47 ...   KxR

48 Q-KN7ch   Resigns

After 48 ... K-R4; 49 Q-R7ch or 48 ... K-B4; 49 Q-Q7ch White wins the Queen.

A very beautiful game, full of fascinating play and ingenious resource. Such keen fighting chess makes a memorable experience for those fortunate enough to play over a true master game. When we become absorbed in masterpieces like this one, we realize what a bountiful store of pleasure is locked up in the games of the great masters.

CHAPTER 5

MASTERPIECES OF THE MASTERS

The Vision and the Plan

PERHAPS you remember the old Greek myth about Ariadne and how she helped Theseus escape from the maze of the Minotaur by placing a colored thread on the floors of the rooms of the palace to guide him to safety.

I am often reminded of this story when students ask, "How do you plan a game of chess? How do you look ahead? How can you foresee what will happen?"

These are good questions, and the answers are not easy. For one thing, all plans must reckon with the opponent's ability to branch off and turn the best plans upside down.

Even for those readers who may perhaps not be doing much playing but are merely interested in enjoying master games, these questions are important. When we play over a game that seems to make sense from start to finish, we are more likely to appreciate it than in the case of a game which seems to proceed by fits and starts.

So again we ask ourselves, "What plan, what vision, does the master bring to a game?"

The answer may seem surprising. Looking ahead and planning seem to call for logical, rigorously exact thinking. But how can anyone be exact when he is confronting the unknown? The game may develop in any one of millions of ways. This nebulous prospect makes a mockery of planning.

And yet the chess player is not entirely helpless. Even at the very beginning of the game he has a guide, and that guide is instinct, faith, a "hunch." Here is the thread of Ariadne which guides him to success.

What do I mean by this? Even at the very start of the game, certain moves are made which imply that the game may take such-and-such a course. The master, knowingly or unknowingly, is guided by these moves; his thoughts are led in appropriate directions. Some players follow these hunches consciously, others are unconsciously led by them.

Sooner or later, when the implications of the earlier moves become obvious, the inarticulate hunch turns into purposeful reasoning. But until the why and wherefore become obvious, the master is content to be guided by the Ariadne thread of instinct.

It takes great poise and experience to acquire this quality of "negative capability," as John Keats called it. He saw it as the ability to endure, "when a man is capable of being in uncertainties, mysteries, doubts, without any irritable reaching after fact and reason." Only an outstanding master, brimming with self-confidence, can allow himself to be guided in this way by a sure but indefinable instinct.

This elusive quality is not an easy one to nail down. Yet there is many a master game in which we can see it at work. For example, the following game, which has three main stages.

In the first stage, the opening, White goes wrong in two ways.

To begin with, he throws away his rightful initiative with the unnecessarily conservative 3 P-K3. This encourages Black to play aggressively.

In this unappetizing situation, White should complete his opening maneuvers with 8 Castles, getting his King into safety. But White misses this point, leaving his King in the center.

Now comes the second stage, starting the middle game with White's vulnerable King in the center. Beginning with 8 ... PxP! Black increases his positional advantage, creates weaknesses in White's game, utilizes the position of White's King for tactical threats, etc.

Black's ferocious threats culminate in 16 ... R-K1! and 17 ... P-KN4! This leads to the third stage: to escape from the threats, White decides to castle, come what may. But Black is well prepared: he shifts at once to the King Knight file, and carries out a brusque attack which is as brilliant as it is forceful.

This game appears as a tour de force of splendid planning and precise timing—all based on White's inexactitudes in the opening.

Kemeri, 1937

QUEEN'S PAWN OPENING

WHITE	BLACK
K. Rellstab	*V. Petrov*
1 P-Q4	P-Q4
2 N-KB3	. . .

White expects 2 ... N-KB3, after which he will take the initiative in the center with 3 P-B4.

But Black forestalls him with:

2 . . .   P-QB4

Is Black justified in trying to seize the initiative in the center? Not really, for White should now play 3 P-B4, making his initiative clear. (*See Diagram 55*)

3 P-K3   . . .

But this puts a different complexion on the matter. Instead of trying to recover the initiative, White plays a quiet defensive move. Thus, at this early stage, Black gets the go-ahead signal for an aggressive policy. The Ariadne thread is already visible!

But there is even more to be learned from White's last move. He has voluntarily deprived his Queen Bishop of its best

Diagram 55 (*White to move*)

BLACK: Petrov

WHITE: Rellstab

diagonal; his King Pawn blocks the development of the Bishop. Here is another guide to the future course of the game. (As a matter of fact, this Bishop never comes to life.)

    3 . . .   N-KB3
    4 B-Q3   P-KN3!

Another significant move. Black intends to develop his King Bishop at King Knight 2, where it will be effectively posted.

Note also that when Black plays ... P-KN3 he breaks the attacking diagonal of White's well-posted Bishop at Queen 3, aimed at Black's future castled position.

Incidentally, Black does not imitate White by playing ... P-K3. Instead, Black keeps the diagonal of his Queen Bishop open and thus allows for the possible development of his Queen Bishop to King Bishop 4 or King Knight 5.

    5 QN-Q2   QN-Q2
    6 P-QN3   . . .

White must find an outlet for his Queen Bishop, which he intends to develop at Queen Knight 2. However, as we shall see, this development is not very satisfactory because the Bishop is blocked by the White Queen Pawn.

    6 . . .   B-N2

7 B-N2   Castles

Now Black intends to free himself still further by playing
... P-K4, despite all the force that White has trained on the
King 5 square!

Diagram 56 (*White to move*)

BLACK: Petrov

WHITE: Rellstab

White's best course is to get his King into safety. After his
illogical third move he has nothing better than to strive for
equality.

After 8 Castles, Black would play the surprising 8 ... P-K4!
Then if 9 PxKP, N-N5! and Black recovers his Pawn with a fine
game, as White's Pawn at King 5 is pinned and cannot be
defended any further.

Comparatively best was 8 Castles, P-K4!; 9 NxP, NxN; 10
PxN, N-N5. Now 11 P-KB4? will not do because of 11 ...
NxP/K6. So White plays 11 N-B3, and after 11 ... Q-B2 Black
must recover his Pawn. There follows 12 P-QB4 (to give White's
forces more playing room), NxKP; 13 NxN, BxN; 14 BxB,
QxB; 15 PxP, QxQP; 16 B-B4 and White can make a fair fight
of it.

Black's instinctive guide (generalized initiative) would then disappear, to be replaced by a concrete positional advantage (Queen-side majority of Pawns). This is a good example of how the initial groping is replaced in time by tangible prospects.

8 P-KR3? ...

But White is too ambitious. He wants to prevent ... N-N5, thereby preventing ... P-K4. What he fails to realize is that Black has other advantageous possibilities. Meanwhile White has weakened his future castled position by advancing his King Rook Pawn.

8 ... PxP!

The period of groping is already over. Black can go ahead to plan on a broad scale.

His last move, for example, was very powerful. If White recaptures by 9 BxP, he gives up the center to Black, who retorts 9 ... Q-B2 followed by 10 ... P-K4 with a magnificent Pawn center.

9 PxP ...

In order to hold the center. But now his Queen Bishop remains buried, and a valuable square beckons to Black's King Knight.

9 ... N-R4!

Black expects 10 Castles, which he will answer with 10 ... N-B5 posting this Knight with splendid effect. Being condemned to passivity, White ought to allow this continuation. Instead, he struggles and flounders.

10 P-N3 ...

He keeps Black's Knight out—but at the cost of further weakening his King-side.

10 ... Q-B2!

Black takes advantage of the new weakness to put a veto on White's castling.

If White replies 11 Castles, there follows 11 ... NxP!; 12 PxN, QxNPch; 13 K-R1, QxPch and Black has a lasting attack plus three Pawns for the sacrificed piece.

Diagram 57 (*White to move*)

BLACK: Petrov

WHITE: Rellstab

11 Q-K2 . . .

White prepares for castling. His idea is to play 12 Castles, when 12 ... NxP? will not do because of 13 PxN, QxNPch; 14 Q-N2 etc.

But Black has an endless series of threats, and proceeds imperturbably with:

11 ... N-B4!

Taking resourceful advantage of the fact that White's Queen Pawn is pinned, and once more underlining the unsatisfactory position of White's Queen Bishop. (White would lose a Pawn after 12 PxN?, BxB; 13 QR-N1, B-R6; 14 P-QN4, P-QR4!.)

Meanwhile Black threatens to win a Pawn by 12 ... NxBch; 13 QxN, B-B4. Or 12 ... NxBch; 13 PxN, Q-B7; 14 B-R3, B-B4, etc.

12 N-K5 NxBch

This leaves White little choice, for if 13 PxN, P-B3; 14 KN-B3, B-R3 White's position would be very awkward. Worse yet, the doubled and isolated Queen Pawn would be a serious and permanent weakness.

13 NxN . . .

Setting a trap: if 13 . . . QxBP??; 14 QR-B1 and Black's Queen is trapped. Naturally Black is too sly to be caught.

13 . . .   B-B4!

Black renews the threat of . . . QxBP. Nor is he afraid of the reply 14 P-KN4, which he can turn to his advantage.

Diagram 58 (*White to move*)

BLACK: Petrov

WHITE: Rellstab

In the event of 14 P-KN4, Black plays 14 . . . BxN, and if 15 QxB, N-B5; 16 Q-QB3, Q-Q3 threatening to win a Pawn by 17 . . . QR-B1. A secondary threat is 17 . . . Q-K3ch forcing White's King to move, for if 18 Q-K3?, N-N7ch winning White's Queen.

Nor will 14 P-KN4, BxN; 15 PxB do, for then comes 15 . . . N-B5; 16 Q-B3, Q-B7; 17 QxN, QxB winning White's Pawn at Queen 4.

14 QR-B1   QR-B1!

Black is fully prepared for 15 P-KN4, BxN; 16 PxB which on the face of it seems to win a piece. There follows 16 . . . QxRch!; 17 BxQ, RxBch; 18 Q-Q1, RxQch and *Black* has won a piece.

Or if 15 P-KN4, BxN; 16 QxB, N-B5; 17 Q-KB3, P-K4! and the opening of the King file is ruinous for White.

15 Q-K3 . . .

There are two reasons for this move. One is that the White Queen is no longer exposed to the eventual attack by ... N-B5. The other reason is that White's King can now go to King 2 if need be.

For example, White threatens 16 P-KN4, BxN; 17 PxB, QxRch; 18 BxQ, RxBch; 19 K-K2, RxR; 20 PxN and White can make a fight of it.

15 . . . Q-Q3! /

Black gets his Queen out of the line of potential attack. The reason why will become clear in the next note.

Diagram 59 (*White to move*)

BLACK: Petrov

WHITE: Rellstab

If now 16 P-KN4, BxN; 17 PxB and Black's Queen is not attacked. There follows 17 ... RxRch; 18 BxR; N-B5 with an overwhelming initiative. (For example 19 Castles?, BxP! and White cannot capture the Bishop because of 20 ... N-K7ch.)

16 P-QB3 R-K1!

A new danger for White. Black threatens ... P-K4! when White would be lost.

17 P-KB4 . . .

Weakening the King-side still more, but he must prevent
... P-K4 at all cost.

17 . . .   P-KN4!

Very fine play. He threatens 18 . . . BxN; 19 QxB, PxP, etc.—
or even 18 . . . PxP; 19 NxP, P-K4! and wins on the King file.

18 Castles   . . .

The pressure is altogether too much for White. He decides
to castle into comparative safety even at the cost of a Pawn:
18 . . . BxRP; 19 R-KB2.

18 . . .   PxP!

Winning the Pawn is too petty for Black. He wants to open
the King Knight file against White's riddled castled position.

19 NxP   . . .

Or 19 PxP, Q-N3ch and Black wins some material.

19 . . .   B-R3!

A useful pin which also helps to clear the open King Knight
file for Black's Rooks.

20 Q-B3   . . .

To get out of the pin.

20 . . .   NxN
21 PxN   K-R1!

Diagram 60 (*White to move*)

BLACK: Petrov

WHITE: Rellstab

Black has his sights firmly fixed on the White King. Black's intended occupation of the open King Knight file cannot be met in force by White, for his King Rook is tied down by the need for defending the weak King Bishop Pawn. This is an indication that Black's powerful Bishops are co-operating usefully in the coming finish. (Note, on the other hand, that White's miserable Bishop is more useless than ever.)

| 22 R-KB2 | R-KN1ch |
| 23 K-R2 | R-N3 |

It is still impossible for White to oppose Rooks on the open file. For example: 24 R-KN1, QR-KN1; 25 RxR, QxR; 26 R-N2, BxPch!! and Black wins a piece (27 K-N1, QxRch; 28 QxQ, BxN, etc.)

| 24 P-B4 | QR-KN1 |

Now White has no defense, for example 25 P-B5, Q-KB3; 26 R-B3, Q-R5; 27 N-B1, B-K5, etc.

| 25 PxP | . . . |

Diagram 61 (*Black to move*)

BLACK: Petrov

WHITE: Rellstab

| 25 . . . | BxPch!! |

If White declines the Bishop, there follows 26 K-R1, R-N6!; 27 QxB, QxQ; 28 RxQ, RxRP mate.

26 QxB   R-N6!!

With the vicious threat of ... RxRP mate.

White resigns, for if 27 QxB, Black plays 27 ... RxRP dbl ch!; 28 KxR, Q-N6 mate—or 27 ... R-N7 dbl ch and mate next move.

Final Position

Diagram 62 (*White to move*)

BLACK: Petrov

WHITE: Rellstab

This is a very fine example of how the initial groping for position gradually blends into purposeful planning and a whole series of powerful threats. The consistency of Black's play is highlighted by the fact that right to the very end, White's unfortunate Queen Bishop remains out of action and useless for any constructive purpose. Black's play from start to finish is a masterpiece of brilliant planning.

The fateful decision

In the game we have just played over, Black had his broad hint of things to come as early as the third move. In many a game enlightenment comes much later, if it comes at all. Then the groping period is drawn out, and logic waits hat in hand while instinct and faith continue to guide the players.

It is in such trying circumstances that a master must rely on his "negative capability." But there is more to it. At any move something decisive *may* happen, the game may be wrenched out of its previous drift, and vague possibilities may be replaced by sharply defined goals.

To perceive these opportunities and to act on them swiftly requires great presence of mind and equally great resilience. But these are only some of the qualities that go into the making of a notable chessmaster.

In the following game White is alert to the change of scene and the resulting kaleidoscopic change of prospects. But Black is not; and the difference, as you will see, turns out to be the difference between winning and losing.

The curious thing about this game is the abrupt transition from the opening to the endgame, as Queens are exchanged on the fifteenth move, shortly after the opening stage.

One of the significant features of the opening is White's 7 P-QN4!?, which looks as if it might lead to a serious weakness in his Queen-side Pawn structure.

The other noteworthy point is that White is unable to castle, thanks to the commanding position of Black's King Bishop.

Black has a promising setup for the middle game by playing 14 ... Q-Q2. Instead he leads into a lost ending with 14 ... BxN? and 15 ... QxQch?

White has a machinelike win which he carries out methodically. Black never has a chance. This ending is a marvelous study in relentless technique.

Leipzig, 1894

KING'S GAMBIT DECLINED

WHITE	BLACK
J. Blackburne	C. Schlechter
1 P-K4	P-K4
2 P-KB4	. . .

The King's Gambit. White offers a Pawn—temporarily as a rule—in order to build up a powerful Pawn center, thanks to the disappearance of Black's King Pawn. In addition, he hopes to develop more rapidly than Black and mount an offensive very quickly along the King Bishop file and along the diagonal from his Queen Bishop 4 to King Bishop 7. (*See Diagram 63*)

In other words, White's second move is one of those crucial moves that embodies a program and can lead to a clearly defined struggle—if Black is so minded.

2 . . .   B-B4

Black has his own ideas on the subject. Rather than submit to passive defense, he prefers his own brand of counterattack. Mind you, he is not passing any judgment on the value of defensive play. He is merely saying, "Passive defense may be all right for other players, but it's not my dish of tea. I prefer a different course."

The abrupt change in the nature of White's planning is clearly brought out in the ancient trap 3 PxP??, Q-R5ch and wins. For if 4 K-K2, QxKP mate. And if 4 P-KN3, QxKPch wins a Rook.

This is a warning to White: "Watch your step. Don't attack too impetuously. Black will have a good development—which means he can hit back hard."

And another problem is shaping up for White. The hostile King Bishop commands the line leading to White's King Knight 1. In other words, *White will be unable to castle until the obnoxious Bishop is disposed of.*

Diagram 63 (*White to move*)

BLACK: Schlechter

WHITE: Blackburne

3 N-KB3	P-Q3

Black is nonchalant about guarding his King Pawn, for on 4 PxP, PxP; 5 NxP he still has the resource of . . . Q-R5ch.

4 B-B4	N-KB3

Development with counterattack on White's King Pawn. Now if 5 PxP, PxP; 6 NxP, Q-Q5! (threatening . . . Q-B7 mate) wins for Black.

5 P-Q3	N-B3
6 P-B3	. . .

This implies some further action against Black's annoying Bishop, possibly by P-Q4 or P-QN4. But Black goes calmly about his business.

6 . . .	Castles
7 P-QN4!?	. . .

White is still unable to castle because of the commanding diagonal of Black's King Bishop. The attack on the Bishop offers no relief, for Black's Bishop does the same work on Queen Knight 3 as it did on Queen Bishop 4. But White apparently reasons that he is in some way on the road to eliminating the obstreperous Bishop.

On the other hand, there are definite drawbacks toward White's Pawn move. It leads to a general weakening of White's Queen-side Pawns.

7 . . .   B-N3

Diagram 64 (*White to move*)

BLACK: Schlechter

WHITE: Blackburne

Another crisis. At first sight it seems that White can win a Pawn with 8 P-N5, N-QR4; 9 PxP.

But in that case Black plays 9 . . . NxP! with a splendid position.

8 P-QR4   . . .

A further weakening of White's Queen-side. The Pawn advance, to be sure, threatens 9 P-R5 winning Black's precious Bishop.

8 . . .   P-QR3

Black creates a flight square for his menaced Bishop.

9 PxP   . . .

An important decision. The development of White's Queen-side is a troublesome problem. He cannot play B-K3, for example. Therefore he plays the text in order to be able to continue with B-KN5. But, as you will see, the move has its drawbacks.

9 . . .   PxP

10 B-KN5   Q-Q3

Black's Queen immediately slips out of the pin on his King Knight.

Diagram 65 (*White to move*)

BLACK: Schlechter

WHITE: Blackburne

Both players have gained by the exchange of Pawns. White has obtained a half-open King Bishop file and developed his Queen Bishop; Black has obtained a half-open Queen file, together with pressure on White's Queen Pawn.

This Pawn, since it cannot be guarded by a Pawn, must be guarded by pieces. True, White's King Bishop now performs that function; but after Black's coming ... B-K3 (followed by ... QR-Q1), White will be embarrassed for a good defense of his Queen Pawn.

Thus a new crisis is shaping up.

11 N-R3   . . .

This is development of a sort. We know that a Knight developed to the side of the board has only minimum mobility. Sooner or later, therefore, this Knight must head for the center. White, as we shall see, intends to bring this Knight to Queen Bishop 4, where it will take a more active part in the game.

11 . . .   N-K2

In order to play ... N-N3 followed by ... P-R3—driving off White's Queen Bishop. White must work fast.

12 B-N3   . . .

Threatening N-B4. The position has become very critical.

12 . . .   B-K3

Expecting 13 BxB, QxB; 14 N-B4, N-N3; 15 NxB, PxN; 16 Castles, QR-B1; 17 Q-Q2, P-R3; 18 BxN, QxB followed by ... KR-Q1 with magnificent pressure against White's weak Pawns.

But White is well prepared.

Diagram 66 (*White to move*)

BLACK: Schlechter

WHITE: Blackburne

13 BxN!   . . .

Perfect timing. The object of this move is to give Black unwieldy doubled King Bishop Pawns (after 13 ... PxB) which may become a serious endgame weakness.

Here is an important point: if Black tries to escape this variation by replying 13 ... BxB (attacking White's Queen), White wins a piece by 14 BxN!

For example: 14 ... BxQ; 15 BxQ, BxN; 16 BxR, BxP; 17

B-B5!, BxR; 18 K-B2 and Black's wandering Bishop is trapped.
Consequently Black's next move is forced.

    13 . . .   PxB
    14 N-B4!?   . . .

A crafty move which gives Black a chance to go wildly wrong.

Black's best course is 14 . . . Q-Q2. True, White can then get
rid of the precious Bishop, but after 15 NxB, PxN he is far from
happy. Thus, 16 Castles? is ruled out because of 16 . . . BxB; 17
QxB, QxQP and Black is a solid Pawn to the good.

If on the other hand 14 . . . Q-Q2; 15 NxB, PxN; 16 BxB,
PxB; 17 Castles, QR-Q1 and White is embarrassed for a suitable
protection for his Queen Pawn.

    14 . . .   BxN?

Black anticipates 15 BxB, after which he simply continues
14 . . . QR-Q1 and White is still unable to castle.

    15 PxB!!   . . .

An amazing rejoinder, which gives the game a wholly new
turn. Come what may, White has now ruled out the annoying
pressure of Black's Bishop. (What has made White's last move
hard to foresee is that he has blocked his own Bishop—but only
for the time being, as we shall see.)

Diagram 67 (*Black to move*)

BLACK: Schlechter

WHITE: Blackburne

White threatens P-B5, freeing his own Bishop and imprisoning Black's Bishop. Of course Black must not play 15 ... P-QB4??? as this would lose his Queen.

The right move is 15 ... B-K6! maintaining freedom for his Bishop, even though after 16 Q-K2, B-R3 the Bishop has had to renounce his best diagonal. Even in that case White's game would have been preferable—but not to the extent that prevails after Black's next move.

> 15 . . .   QxQch?

Black is asleep. Completely unaware of the crisis, he condemns himself to lasting passivity.

> 16 RxQ   . . .

Black cannot prevent the coming P-B5. Thus after 16 ... P-QB4 White has 17 R-Q6, B-B2 (if 17 ... B-Q1; 18 RxBP is feasible); 18 R-Q7! (not 18 RxBP?, K-N2 and White's Rook is trapped), B-Q1; 19 RxNP and White has a winning endgame.

> 16 . . .   QR-Q1

If 16 ... P-B3, 17 R-Q7 wins a valuable Pawn.

> 17 P-B5!   . . .

White has achieved the first objective of his grand strategical plan: he has banished the Black Bishop to outer darkness.

> 17 . . .   RxRch
> 18 KxR   R-Q1ch
> 19 K-K2   B-R2
> 20 P-R5!   . . .

A brilliant idea. If Black tries to liberate his Bishop with 20 ... P-N3 there follows 21 RPxP, PxP; 22 R-R1! with decisive positional advantage for White.

White's Queen-side Pawns are no longer potential weaknesses; there is no way for Black to exploit them.

Since White's Bishop can be put to use while Black's Bishop is out of play, White is in effect operating with a piece to the good.

Diagram 68 (*Black to move*)

BLACK: Schlechter

WHITE: Blackburne

Black is limited to passive resistance. The interesting aspect of the following play is this: will White find a convincing winning plan?

20 . . .		P-B3
21 R-KB1		N-N3
22 P-N3!		. . .

To prevent . . . N-B5ch. White is bent on systematically reducing the mobility of enemy pieces.

22 . . .		B-N1

Black has four weak Pawns: his Queen Knight Pawn, his King Bishop Pawns, and his King Rook Pawn. None of these Pawns can be defended by Pawns; they *must* be defended by pieces. Consequently they are all legitimate targets for White's attack.

How is White to attack the weak Pawns? The most powerful possibility is to bring his Bishop to Queen Bishop 8, winning Black's Queen Knight Pawn to begin with. But as long as Black's Rook is on the board, White's Bishop maneuver is impossible. *Therefore, White must exchange Rooks in order to menace the weak Pawns.*

Diagram 69 (*White to move*)

BLACK: Schlechter

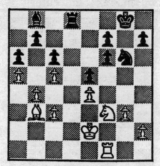

WHITE: Blackburne

Further facets of White's plans will unfold as the play goes
on. But even at this point we can sense how enjoyable it is to
study the master's beautifully effective method of solving a
problem that would baffle lesser players.

23 N-Q2   . . .

By moving his Knight, White attacks a Pawn. However, that
is not the main point of the move. By playing N-B4 White will
have this piece poised for N-Q6, menacing White's weak Queen
Knight Pawn. Then, if Black plays . . . BxN, the ensuing PxB
gives White a mighty passed Pawn that wins quickly.

But this, too, calls for the exchange of Rooks.

23 . . .	K-N2
24 N-B4	N-K2
25 N-K3	B-B2
26 R-Q1!	. . .

Pointing a dagger at Black's breast. Black can evade the
exchange of Rooks only at the cost of allowing the murderous
invasion R-Q7.

If Black plays 26 . . . R-QN1 there follows 27 R-Q7!, B-Q1;
28 N-B4 followed by 29 N-Q6 and Black can resign.

Diagram 70 (*Black to move*)

BLACK: Schlechter

WHITE: Blackburne

26 . . .   RxR
27 BxR!   . . .

The Bishop heads for the right diagonal. White will soon play
B-N4 (when that move becomes possible), heading for Queen
Bishop 8. Thus White's plans begin to take solid shape.

In the long run, as we shall see, Black is helpless against this
threat.

Diagram 71 (*Black to move*)

BLACK: Schlechter

WHITE: Blackburne

Here is what happens if Black tries to prevent White's Bishop from reaching Knight 4: 27 ... K-N3; 28 N-B4. Now White threatens 29 N-Q6, BxN; 30 PxB and the Pawn queens by force! So Black plays 28 ... N-B1 to stop the invasion.

Now comes 29 K-K3 (threatening B-N4).

Black plays 29 ... P-R4 to prevent the Bishop move. White then forces the issue with 30 P-R3!

White must then win, for example 30 ... B-N1; 31 P-N4!, P-R5; 32 P-N5!, KxP; 33 B-N4, N-K2; 34 N-Q6 and wins.

Or suppose Black tries 30 ... K-N4, in which case White wins with 31 P-R4ch, K-N3; 32 P-N4!, PxP; 33 BxP, N-K2; 34 N-Q6.

Here we have the blueprint for White's coming victory. Before you go on with the actual game, study these variations thoroughly until you have mastered them.

| 27 ... | K-B1 |

Black heads to the Queen-side with his King, in order to be able to prevent the eventual B-B8. But this leaves his vulnerable King-side Pawns at the mercy of White's King.

White's ensuing King maneuver (K-Q3-B4) contributes nothing to the winning process; he wastes some time until he puts together all the elements needed for victory.

28 K-Q3	K-K1
29 B-N4	K-Q1
30 N-B5!	. . .

(*See Diagram 72*)

If now 30 ... NxN; 31 BxN, P-R3. In that event, Black's King is tied to its present square, for a King move would allow B-B8 winning at least two Pawns. White can therefore do the following: (1) bring his King to King Rook 5; (2) capture Black's King Rook Pawn; (3) advance his newly passed King Rook Pawn and queen it.

Black consequently avoids the exchange of Knights.

Diagram 72 (*Black to move*)

BLACK: Schlechter

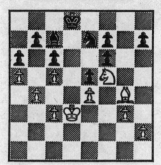

WHITE: Blackburne

30 . . .	N-N1
31 K-B4	. . .

White can save a little time by playing K-K3 directly.

31 . . .	B-N1
32 B-R3	. . .

Black has little choice now. If for example 32 ... N-K2?; 33 NxN, KxN; 34 B-B8 wins.

32 . . .	B-B2
33 K-Q3	. . .

White has the right idea. His King heads for King Rook 5.

33 . . .	B-N1
34 K-K3	B-B2
35 K-B3	. . .

(*See Diagram 73*)

Black is still helpless. If he tries to prevent K-N4 by playing 35 ... P-R4, White can win in a variety of ways. The simplest is 36 N-N7, winning the King Rook Pawn.

35 . . .	B-N1
36 K-N4	B-B2

Diagram 73 (*Black to move*)

BLACK: Schlechter

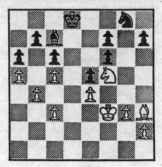

WHITE: Blackburne

    37 K-R5   . . .

The ideal position for White. If now 37 ... B-N1; 38 N-Q6 and White wins as in the actual game.

    37 . . .   K-K1
    38 N-Q6ch   BxN
    39 PxB   K-Q1

Forced. White threatened B-B8.

    40 B-B5!   Resigns

A beautiful finish. If 40 ... P-R3; 41 B-R7 wins the Knight! Or if 40 ... K-K1; 41 BxP, K-B1; 42 BxN, KxB; 43 P-Q7 and the Pawn queens. (*See Diagram 74*)

With the benefit of hindsight, we can see that White had a won game after Black's faulty fifteenth move. What made the further play an enchanting study for us was that White carried out his plan inexorably, without forceful or violent moves. Merely by the power of pure thought he ground Black down and crushed his powers of resistance.

Thus we have a perfect example here of a winning plan based on an accurate appraisal of the possibilities inherent in a given

Final Position

Diagram 74 (*Black to move*)

BLACK: Schlechter

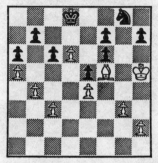

WHITE: Blackburne

position. But what is even more fascinating is the way that White exploited Black's failure to see the winning plan. Up to the fifteenth White had nothing concrete on which to base a winning plan. As soon as Black made a severe strategical blunder, the period of groping was at an end. Reason and logic took over, and almost every move was suggested to White by his allegiance to an over-all winning plan that proved irresistible.

Master chess abounds in such games in which a logical plan triumphs over all opposition. When we play over games like this one, we feel that chess is both an art and a science. This realization gives us an enormously enhanced pleasure, for we well know that we could never experience an equally keen satisfaction from our own muddled games.

CHAPTER 6

THE ANATOMY OF A MASTERPIECE

The Fascination of the Middle Game

CHESS is interesting all the way, from the early struggle for position in the opening, right down to the delicate calcu-
lations of the endgame. Nevertheless, the middle game, with its
complex possibilities and exciting hand-to-hand struggles, *is*
chess—chess at its most thrilling and absorbing.

The middle game may be said to start about the tenth move
or so, when both players have brought out quite a few pieces
and are ready to attack, maneuver, and make constructive plans.
Should the Queens be exchanged, we find ourselves in the
endgame stage.

What makes the middle game so rich in possibilities is the
presence of the Queens on the board. Since the Queen has by
far the most powerful range of any of the pieces, its presence
makes possible the most far-reaching maneuvers, the most aggressive plans, the most brilliant combinations.

Although we do not often stop to think of it, success or failure
in the middle game hinges on the effectiveness of the Queens.
When a player wins by forceful conduct of the middle game,
you may be sure his Queen was right in the thick of the fight.
On the other hand, you will find that the loser's Queen played
a miserable role. Either this piece had little scope, or else it was
far from the scene of action.

127

In other words, success or failure in the middle game is generally determined by the *qualitative* strength of the Queen. The player who gets the utmost power out of the Queen's tremendous range is the player who gets the decision in the middle game. The player who neglects the Queen's powers or doesn't know how to put them to the best use—he's the predestined loser.

The ticking of the watch

In the following game we have a good example of the way in which powerful handling of the Queen assures victory in the middle game; whereas the loser's Queen plays a miserable role all the way.

White is well aware of the power of the Queen and how to apply that power with utmost effectiveness. This master was so systematic in making use of an advantage that someone described the winning process as reminding him of the ticking of a watch.

White brings the Queen to a formidable post and then steadily improves his position move by move. In the end he finds the maximum use for his Queen—sacrificing it for an even greater advantage! Such reasoning is paradoxical and yet quite logical: powerful as the Queen is, there are situations which are even more advantageous than one in which the Queen lords it over the enemy position.

White immediately demonstrates the soundness of the Queen sacrifice, forcing Black's resignation in a few more moves.

FOUR KNIGHTS' GAME

Ostend, 1907

WHITE	BLACK
S. Tarrasch	D. Janowski
1 P-K4	P-K4
2 N-KB3	N-QB3
3 N-B3	N-B3

This leads to a slow kind of opening, with leisurely development and a delay in coming to grips. Very often the symmetrical character of the opening persists for quite a while.

This slow build-up paradoxically puts a premium on alertness. It often happens in this opening that the player who perceives an opportunity to take a slight initiative gets distinctly the better game.

4 B-N5   B-N5

Diagram 75 (White to move)

BLACK: Janowski

WHITE: Tarrasch

Any attempt on White's part to win a Pawn doesn't work. An interesting example is: 5 BxN, QPxB; 6 NxP. Now Black retaliates with 6 ... NxP; 7 NxN, Q-Q5 and Black wins one of the Knights, drawing even in material once more.

5 Castles   Castles

And here 6 BxN, QPxB; 7 NxP, BxN; 8 QPxB, NxP leads to a dull position in which White's hopes of winning would be microscopic. In the eyes of an enterprising player, such soulless simplification would be a betrayal of the spirit of the middle game. Consequently White avoids exchanges in his search for a rich, complex, lively middle game.

6 P-Q3   . . .

Now that White's King Pawn is securely protected, he is really threatening 7 BxN, QPxB; 8 NxP with a clear Pawn to the good.

6 . . .   P-Q3

Now Black's King Pawn is firmly guarded as well.

7 B-N5   . . .

This move, involving a pin that may become burdensome for Black, at last promises some action. The possibility of White's N-Q5 spells potential trouble for Black; the minimum result would be the ripping up of the Pawns in front of his King.

Diagram 76 (Black to move)

BLACK: Janowski

WHITE: Tarrasch

The simplest way for Black to dispose of the threat of N-Q5 is to play . . . BxN. In this case Black, who is fond of retaining the two Bishops, selects a more complicated course.

7 . . .   N-K2

This takes the sting out of N-Q5 and also prepares for . . . P-B3. Meanwhile White's Bishop at Queen Knight 5, left standing in mid-air as it were, makes a rather futile impression.

The position is not an easy one for White to handle. Standard procedure here would be for him to play BxN, breaking up the castled Pawn position. But this procedure is ineffective at this point, as Black's remaining Knight moves to King Knight 3 and shields the castled King quite efficiently.

Diagram 77 (*White to move*)

BLACK: Janowski

WHITE: Tarrasch

Here are the likely consequences of 8 BxN; PxB. White continues 9 N-KR4 in order to play P-B4 opening the King Bishop file for action against Black's castled position. Black plays 9 ... N-N3, practically forcing 10 NxN. But after 10 ... RPxN; 11 P-B4, B-QB4ch; 12 K-R1, K-N2! followed by ... R-R1 Black has two good Bishops and an attack on the open King Rook file, while his King is perfectly safe.

White therefore concludes that 8 BxN would be distinctly premature, and tries a different way:

        8 N-KR4   ...

Now if 8 ... N-N3; 9 NxN, RPxN; 10 P-B4! with a strong initiative for White, who can open the King Bishop file to strengthen his pin on Black's Knight.

        8 ...   P-B3

        9 B-QB4   ...

And here Black can maintain a good position by 9 ... P-Q4; 10 B-N3, Q-Q3 with considerable freedom of action.

Instead, Black plays an inferior move.

9 . . .	B-N5

Waste of time.

10 P-B3	B-K3

Black expects 11 BxB, PxB with a good game for Black, who has opened the King Bishop file.

Diagram 78 (*White to move*)

BLACK: Janowski

WHITE: Tarrasch

But White has a little surprise in store for his opponent, which gives the game quite a different turn.

11 BxN!	. . .

If now 11 . . . BxB? White wins a piece with 12 BxN!, QxB; 13 N-B5! etc.

11 . . .	PxB
12 BxB	PxB

The point of the sequence selected by White is that Black does *not* have an open King Bishop file, and his King is exposed to attack.

13 P-B4	. . .

Already threatening 14 Q-N4ch, K-B2; 15 PxP, QPxP; 16 Q-N5 with an easy win.

13 . . .	N-N3

Black tries to shield his King from hard knocks, but the attempt is not quite successful.

	14 NxN	PxN
	15 Q-N4!	. . .

The double attack on the Black Pawns spells trouble for Black. If he tries 15 ... K-B2, White has a murderous (and obvious) winning line in 16 R-B3 followed by QR-KB1 and PxP.

15 . . .   Q-K1

Contrast the respective positions of the two Queens. White's Queen is aggressive, menacing, poised for action. Black's Queen is purely defensive and has hardly any scope. The *qualitative* difference in the situation of the two Queens spells victory for White, defeat for Black.

Diagram 79 (*White to move*)

BLACK: Janowski

WHITE: Tarrasch

16 P-B5!   . . .

The strongest continuation of White's attack, taking advantage of the fact that Black's King Knight Pawn is pinned. In fact, thanks to the superior mobility of the White Queen, White will soon win a Pawn.

16 . . .   KPxP

17 PxP   BxN

Black throws excess baggage overboard, as his Bishop is less likely to be useful than White's Knight.

18 PxB   . . .

And now 18 . . . P-KN4 will not do because of 19 P-KR4! winning a Pawn and maintaining the attack. The combination of Black's weakened King-side and White's powerful Queen is disastrous for Black.

18 . . .   K-N2

19 R-B3!   . . .

Simple and strong, and preparing for the eventual QR-KB1. White's immediate threat is 20 R-N3, P-KN4; 21 P-KR4 winning.

19 . . .   R-R1

In order to answer 20 R-N3 with 20 . . . R-R3. But this leaves another weakness which White spots relentlessly.

20 PxP!   . . .

For if now 20 . . . QxP; 21 Q-Q7ch is decisive.

Diagram 80 (*Black to move*)

BLACK: Janowski

WHITE: Tarrasch

White's last move was obvious enough, but its value can only be demonstrated by a subtle line of play that Black sees—and avoids.

To wit—what happens if Black plays 20 ... R-R3 in order to recover his Pawn? Here is White's brilliant retort: 21 RxP!!, KxR; 22 R-KB1ch, K-N2 (or 22 ... K-K2; 23 Q-N5ch and White wins easily); 23 R-B7ch, QxR (if 23 ... K-N1; 24 Q-N5, R-R1; 25 Q-B6 and it's all over); 24 PxQ dis ch, KxP; 25 Q-Q7ch and Black's Rooks are no match for White's savagely marauding Queen.

20 ...	Q-K2

Foreseeing White's coming QR-KB1, Black brings up reinforcements for his sickly King Bishop Pawn.

Meanwhile Black is philosophical about the loss of his Knight Pawn. White's far-advanced Pawn, he reasons, merely blocks White's avenues of attack, and Black's King can hide snugly behind the advanced White Pawn.

But White will have something to say about that!

21 P-KR4	...

In order to play P-R5, definitively holding on to his advanced Pawn.

21 ...	P-Q4
22 QR-KB1	QR-KB1
23 P-R5	R-R3

All according to plan. Black has nothing to do but "wait and see."

In order to make headway, White must break through with P-N4 followed by P-N5.

24 R/B1-B2!	R/R3-R1
25 Q-B5!	Q-Q3

(*See Diagram 81*)

26 P-N4!	...

To the threat of P-N5, with a crashing breakthrough, Black

Diagram 81 (*White to move*)

BLACK: Janowski

WHITE: Tarrasch

has no good reply, for instance 26 ... K-R3; 27 P-N7!, KxNP; 28 Q-N6 mate.

Or 26 ... R-R3; 27 P-N5!, RxRP; 28 PxPch, K-R3; 29 R-R3!, RxR; 30 QxRch, KxP; 31 R-N2ch and wins (this check was made possible by White's innocent-looking 24th move). One possible variation is 31 ... KxP; 32 Q-R6ch, K-K2; 33 R-N7ch and wins. Another is 31 ... K-B2; 32 R-N7ch, K-K1; 33 Q-B8ch, Q-Q1; 34 R-K7 mate.

Again and again we see how the fearsome agility of White's Queen decides the game in his favor.

26 ...   Q-K2

27 P-N5!   ...

The long-awaited move that smashes the flimsy barrier Black has set up. But what does White do if Black replies ... PxP attacking the White Queen?

27 ...   PxP

28 QxRch!   ...

The last valuable service performed by the Queen.

28 ...   RxQ

29 RxR   ...

Diagram 82 (*Black to move*)

BLACK: Janowski

WHITE: Tarrasch

White threatens 30 R/B2-B7ch coming out a Rook ahead. If Black tries 29 ... Q-Q3 we get 30 R/B2-B7ch, K-R3; 31 R-R7 mate or 31 R-KR8 mate.

And if 29 ... Q-B4 (to pin White's Rook at King Bishop 2), White forces the win with 30 P-Q4! breaking the pin.

29 . . .   QxR!?

A gallant try, for after 30 RxQ?, KxR; 31 P-R6, P-N5! (or 31 ... P-K5!) the King and Pawn ending would be drawn. For example 31 ... P-N5!; 32 K-B2, P-K5!; 33 PxP, PxP. Now if 34 K-N3, P-K6! or 34 K-K3, P-N6! In either case White must not capture the Pawn and thus the position is a draw.

30 P-R6ch!!   . . .

This long-foreseen resource crushes Black's hopes. If now 30 ... K-N1; 31 P-R7ch, K-N2; 32 RxQ and if Black captures the Queen, White queens his Rook Pawn.

Black therefore resigns.

A delightful game, in which the magnificent deployment of White's Queen leads to highly enjoyable play.

But there are other types of thrills we can get out of a well-played middle game. What of those positions in which a player manages to save a seemingly lost position by means of highly ingenious play?

Teetering on the edge of disaster

"Depend upon it, sir," says Dr. Johnson, "when a man knows he is to be hanged in a fortnight, it concentrates his mind wonderfully." This interesting statement is debatable, for many a man confronted with disaster goes to pieces. How many games have we seen in which one of the players is so overcome by the crisis that he loses his head completely?

So common is this experience, as a matter of fact, that we prize especially those games in which a player, on being confronted with a desperate situation, reacts courageously and resourcefully. The game that follows is so rich in dazzling finesses that it has become an unforgettable masterpiece of its kind.

KING'S INDIAN DEFENSE
Palestine Championship, 1939

WHITE	BLACK
O. Winz	M. Czerniak
1 P-Q4	N-KB3
2 P-QB4	P-KN3
3 P-B3	. . .

White immediately announces that he intends to build a formidable Pawn center. The chances are that once he sets up this center with P-K4, Black's pieces will have little mobility in the center and his game will become restricted.

3 . . .	P-Q4!?

Black hits back in the center, but even this aggressive policy involves Black in difficulties.

| 4 PxP | NxP |
| 5 P-K4 | . . . |

So White means to monopolize the center after all.

5 . . .	N-N3

Diagram 83 (*White to move*)

BLACK: Czerniak

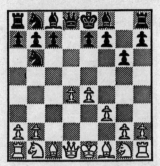

WHITE: Winz

Black retreated his Knight to Queen Knight 3 in order to give his fianchettoed Bishop a clear diagonal when it goes to King Knight 2. (Black's counterplay must rest on pressure against White's Pawn center.)

But at its present post Black's King Knight is awkwardly posted and soon becomes a further target for attack.

6	N-B3	B-N2
7	B-K3	Castles

Black hopes to undermine White's center with 8 ... P-K4; 9 P-Q5, P-QB3. So White prevents ... P-K4.

8	P-B4	N-B3

In order to provoke the advance of White's Queen Pawn, which results in a loosening of White's center. Meanwhile Black loses valuable time.

9	P-Q5	N-N1
10	P-QR4	...

So that after the expected 10 ... P-QB3 he can drive off Black's unfortunate Knight with 11 P-R5. This goads Black to seek risky counterplay.

10	...	P-K4!?
11	P-R5	PxP!?

Diagram 84 (*White to move*)

BLACK: Czerniak

WHITE: Winz

Black hopes for 12 BxP, N/N3-Q2; 13 N-B3, Q-K2 followed by ... N-K4 with a good game, thanks to Black's command of his King 4 square. But White chooses a much more vigorous line which seems to leave Black with a lost game.

       12 PxN!   PxB

       13 RxP!   ...

What a predicament for Black! His Queen Rook is menaced, and if he plays 13 ... RxR?? White queens his Rook Pawn after 14 PxR.

       13 ...   Q-R5ch!!

With this sly possibility: 14 K-K2?, Q-B7ch; 15 K-Q3, N-Q2!!, 16 RxR, N-K4ch; 17 K-Q4, P-K7 discovered check and mate!

But White chooses the obvious and safer alternative.

       14 P-KN3   ...

Now Black's Queen is attacked—yet he has a way out.

       14 ...   BxNch!

       15 PxB   QxKP!

Diagram 85 (*White to move*)

BLACK: Czerniak

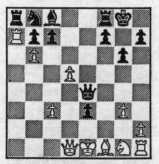

WHITE: Winz

With commendable ingenuity Black has found a way to keep afloat.

If White takes the obvious course and snips pieces, Black can hold his own, for example 16 RxR, QxR (where did that come from?); 17 RxN, QxN (threatening mate!) 18 Q-K2, B-N5!; 19 RxRch, KxR; 20 PxP! (White has a trick or two up *his* sleeve), BxQ; 21 P-B8/Qch, K-N2; 22 KxB, Q-B7ch and Black draws!

If White proceeds more cautiously with 16 Q-B3, Black hits back with 16 ... Q-N8ch! and White has nothing better than 17 Q-Q1, Q-K5! for if 18 K-K2?, RxR; 19 PxR, Q-R7ch and Black has a winning attack.

16 N-B3!   B-N5!

If White stops now to guard his Knight, Black replies ... N-Q2 with a satisfactory game.

17 RxR!   BxN
18 Q-Q3!   . . .

Diagram 86 (*Black to move*)

BLACK: Czerniak

WHITE: Winz

Black can actually come out a piece ahead by playing 18 ... QxQ; 19 BxQ, BxR; but then 20 PxP wins for White: when the Knight moves, White plays 21 RxRch followed by queening his Pawn.

18 . . .   Q-K4

19 PxP!   . . .

This gives Black another chance to go wrong, for if now 19 ... BxR; 20 P-Q6! (shutting off Black's Queen) and again White queens his Pawn and wins too much material.

19 . . .   QxP/B2!

Black chooses the safe way. With one Pawn for the Exchange, he still has an uphill fight.

20 R-N1   Q-N3

Now Black apparently threatens to win by ... P-K7.

(*See Diagram 87*)

White should meet the threat by 21 B-K2. The indicated continuation would be 21 ... Q-N7; 22 QxP (not 22 BxB, Q-KB7ch), BxB; 23 QxB, QxPch; 23 K-B1! with a dour struggle in prospect.

Diagram 87 (*White to move*)

BLACK: Czerniak

WHITE: Winz

21 P-N4? . . .

In effect, White is saying: "You had better win back the Exchange by 21 . . . P-K7; 22 QxB, QxR; 23 QxKP."

This is not particularly inviting for Black, but he must also think of the possibility of R-N3 with unpleasant hounding of his Bishop.

21 . . . R-Q1!

After this clever move, Black's attack flames up all over again. (*See Diagram 88*)

Black threatens 22 . . . RxP winning White's Queen because of the latent threat of . . . R-Q8 mate.

Worse yet, White cannot defend with 22 P-B4?? for then 22 . . . Q-N5ch forces mate next move.

Even 22 Q-N5? will not do, for after 22 . . . RxP!!; 23 RxNch, K-N2 Black still wins.

And on 22 R-QR1, Q-N7! attacks the Rook and also threatens . . . Q-KB7 mate.

Finally, if 22 B-K2, RxP!!; 23 RxNch, K-N2; 24 Q-B2, R-Q7 Black still wins.

Diagram 88 (*White to move*)

BLACK: Czerniak

WHITE: Winz

White seems to have come off very well, as he has a formal advantage in material.

22 R-N3	RxP!!	
23 RxNch	K-N2	
24 RxB	...	

White resigns himself to the inevitable.

24 ...	RxQ	
25 BxR	...	

Diagram 89 (*Black to move*)

BLACK: Czerniak

WHITE: Winz

But now Black reveals that he has seen further ahead, and forces the win of White's Bishop. What follows is a perfect study in the art of exploiting the incoherent relationship of White's disjointed units.

25 . . .	Q-B2!
26 R-K8	QxBPch
27 K-B1	. . .

Realizing that 27 K-K2 is futile because of 27 . . . Q-Q7ch. (Black had to foresee this when he made his 21st move!)

| 27 . . . | QxBch |
| 28 K-N2 | Q-Q7ch |

Diagram 90 (*White to move*)

BLACK: Czerniak

WHITE: Winz

Black gives his opponent no time to catch his breath. If now 29 K-R3, P-R4! when White must not play 30 PxP?? because of 30 . . . Q-Q2ch winning a Rook. And if White tries 30 R/B3xKP, then 30 . . . PxPch leaves Black far ahead in material with an easy win.

| 29 K-N3 | P-K7 |
| 30 R/B3-K3 | . . . |

Just in the nick of time. White can now win the dangerous King Pawn, but Black has another asset—his Queen Knight

Pawn, which will soon start advancing toward the queening square. Black will combine this threat with checks that menace the White King's existence.

30 . . .	Q-K8ch
31 K-R3	Q-KB8ch
32 K-N3	Q-KN8ch
33 K-R3	Q-B7!!

Diagram 91 (*White to move*)

BLACK: Czerniak

WHITE: Winz

If White now plays the obvious 34 RxP, he finds himself in a mating net after 34 . . . Q-B6ch; 35 K-R4, P-R3 (threatening 36 . . . P-KN4ch; 37 K-R5, Q-KR6 mate).

Then if White tries 36 R/K8-K3 there follows 36 . . . P-KN4ch; 37 K-R5, Q-KB3 and Black winds up with . . . Q-KN3 mate.

Or if 36 P-N5, Black concludes neatly with 36 . . . PxPch; 37 KxP, P-B3ch; 38 K-R4, P-KN4 mate.

34 R/K8-K5	P-QN4!
35 P-N5	. . .

Hoping to squelch the mate threat, but it now breaks out in a different form.

Diagram 92 (*Black to Move*)

BLACK: Czerniak

WHITE: Winz

35 . . .   P-R4!

Threatens 36 . . . P-K8/Q; 37 RxQ, Q-B6ch; 38 K-R4, Q-N5 mate.

If White captures the Pawn in passing, we get 36 PxP e.p.ch, KxP and Black threatens to win by 37 . . . P-K8/Q; 38 RxQ, Q-B6ch; 39 K-R4, P-B3 and Black is helpless against the coming . . . P-N4 mate.

Finally, if 36 PxP e.p.ch, KxP; 37 R/K5-K4, P-B4 and Black wins, as he continues with . . . P-N4, etc.

36 R/K5-K4   P-N5!

After a threat on the King-side comes a threat on the other wing. Black simply intends to march his Queen Knight Pawn down to the queening square.

37 RxKP   Q-B6ch
38 K-R4   P-N6

This is getting serious. The Queen Knight Pawn will cost White a Rook, as . . . P-N7 is now threatened.

39 R/K2-K3   Q-B7ch
40 K-R3   P-N7

If now 41 R-K1, Q-B6ch; 42 K-R4, P-N8/Q; 43 RxQ, QxRch; 44 K-N3, QxR and wins.

41 R-K8!?   . . .

Diagram 93 (Black to move)

BLACK: Czerniak

WHITE: Winz

White has no resource left but his sense of humor. He hopes for 41 ... P-N8/Q?? allowing him to play 42 R-KN8 ch!!, KxR; 43 R-K8ch, K-N2; 44 R-KN8ch!!, KxR and White, with two Queens down, is stalemated!

But Black knows a trick worth two of that.

41 . . .   QxRch!

White resigns, as his stalemate threat has evaporated.

With this thrilling game we conclude our little jaunt through the delightful world of master chess. The whole vast range of chess literature is open to you, and you are free to browse through thousands of other enjoyable games. Here is a lifetime of pleasure, of discovery, and rediscovery.

There is literally no limit to the amount of pleasure you can get from playing over the games of the masters. The realm of master chess is like Tennyson's "world whose margin fades / Forever and forever when I move." There are no fixed horizons in this world. No matter how many games delight you, there will always be new ones to provide new surprises, new thrills, new sacrifices, new flashes of genius.

This is a world which is rich in rewards, one in which failure and bitterness and disappointment are ruled out; a world in which old age or poor health does not dim the reader's enjoyment of the endlessly unfolding beauties of master chess.

As time goes on and you become familiar with more fine games, you pick up a repertoire of old favorites that you will want to play over again and again. Each time your pleasure will be renewed, and each time you will find some attractive element that you overlooked in a previous reading. Such games always entertain and never disappoint.

CHAPTER 7

HIT 'EM WHERE THEY AIN'T

The Role of Imagination in Chess

IN the previous chapters you have been thrilled again and again by the unexpected, by the "impossible" being transformed into the possible, the powerful, the decisive stroke. Imagination is the salt and savor of chess. Imagination in chess gives us a heady sense of power; after all, what can be more thrilling, more satisfying, than achieving the "impossible"?

In chess, as in life, imagination quickens our interests, creates new objectives, enhances our zest in living. It is true that orderly method and a systematic approach are valuable aids in playing chess well; yet they are by no means the whole story. If the enlivening imagination is absent from chess, we run a terrifying danger—may not this entrancing game cloy and pall on us in due time?

But remember this: imagination must be stimulated and enriched. Imagination does not exist in a void; it is derived from our knowledge and our memory. The more we learn about chess, the more we study it, the more intensely we enjoy it, the more we add to that store of knowledge and memory that will feed the imagination.

More than one great scientist has observed that outstanding discoveries come from the *new* arrangement of *familiar* elements. And in that respect the chess player is like the scientist: the more he knows, the more material he has to work on in order to produce delightful sacrifices, sparkling combinations, amazing resources in desperate positions, startlingly effective plans in seemingly sterile situations.

Blind Spots

One way to appreciate the value of imagination is to see what happens when it is absent! In chess on any level, such blind spots are disastrous. Take this maddening example from a tournament game played at Kecskemét in 1927:

Diagram 94 (*White to move*)

BLACK: Kmoch

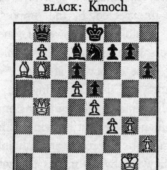

WHITE: Mueller

White is a Pawn ahead—and what a Pawn! It is the protected, far advanced passed Pawn at Queen Knight 7. With his Queen and Bishops perfectly poised for helping the Pawn on, White can win at once with 1 B-B7!! forcing Black to yield the queening square: 1 ... QxB; 2 P-N8/Qch and Black can resign.

Instead White played:

        1 B-R7??   QxBch

White thought there was no distinction between 1-B-B7!! and 1 B-R7?? overlooking the possibility of CHECK!

        2 K-R1   Q-N1

Now the passed Pawn can no longer queen. However, such is its power that White was able to draw the game eventually.

Chess literature abounds in cases of players who are stricken deaf, dumb, and blind in an easily won position. This example, from the German Junior Championship of 1956, is particularly amusing.

Diagram 95 (*Black to move*)

BLACK: Pesch

WHITE: Kestler

With a piece to the good, Black should win fairly easily by 1 ... N-B3.

Instead, blinded by what he considers a sure-fire winning method, Black plays:

1 ...	R-K2???

Expecting 2 Q-R3, Q-N8ch; 3 K-Q2, Q-K8 mate.

2 R-R8ch!	K-R2
3 R-R8ch!!!	KxR
4 Q-KR6ch!!!	QxQ
Drawn	

White is stalemated!

In the next position (from a game at Bad Homburg, 1949) White doesn't come off too badly, as he wins in a won position. What more do we expect of him? We expect him to win in the easiest and quickest way—and this he fails to do, because his mind is completely set on the inferior method.

Diagram 96 (*White to move*)

BLACK: Amateur

WHITE: Bethge

White's actual winning method is ingenious, to be sure:

        1 RxP!?   RxP

Of course if 1 . . . RxR; 2 P-N5ch!!, K-N2; 3 P-K8/Q wins.

        2 K-B6!   . . .

Attacking Black's Rook and also threatening 3 R-KR2 mate.

        2 . . .   R-K7!?

A nice try: if 2 RxR? Black is stalemated.

        3 P-N5ch!   Resigns

For after 3 . . . K-R4; 4 RxR White's material advantage wins easily.

All very neat, but look at this winning method (from Diagram 96):

        1 P-N5ch!   K-R4

If 1 . . . K-N2; 2 P-K8/Q dis ch wins at once.

        2 P-K8/Qch!   RxQ

3 RxRP mate!

All neat, forced, and pretty. Despite its simplicity, this pretty winning line is hard to see because White "gives away" his precious passed Pawn at move 2.

Chess blindness in winning positions can be annoying. In defensive positions it is generally disastrous, as in the following game played at Berlin in 1934.

Diagram 97 (*White to move*)

BLACK: Amateur

WHITE: Kunnemann

White is a Pawn down, and is on the point of losing a second one. He must therefore make the most of his chances by playing:

1 RxB!	RxR
2 Q-B6	. . .

Threatening mate and attacking the Rook as well.

2 . . .	Q-N8ch!
3 K-N2	Q-K5ch

White must now take a draw by 4 K-N1, Q-N8ch (or 4 . . . Q-K8ch); 5 K-N2, Q-K5ch, etc.

If 4 K-R3?, Q-B4ch wins for Black. And if 4 P-B3?, Q-B7ch wins for Black.

But White is not content with a draw; he tries a grand swindle in the well-founded hope of dazzling his opponent and striking him with chess blindness. So (from Diagram 97):

> 1 Q-B6!?   ...

Black sees that this move threatens RxB. He even sees that 1 ... BxQ?? will not do because of 2 R-K8 mate. Whereupon he complacently plays:

> 1 ...   QxBP??

Protecting the Bishop. But here's what White didn't see:

> 2 Q-N7ch!!   BxQ
> 3 R-K8ch   B-B1
> 4 RxB mate

But there's more to it. Once more going back to Diagram 97, let's look at the winning defense that both players missed:

> 1 Q-B6!?   Q-B8!!

This beautiful move paralyzes White's attack. If 2 RxQ, BxQ is feasible. Or if 2 BxQ, BxQ is again possible. Finally, since White's Rook is pinned, White cannot dream of playing 2 Q-N7ch. But both players were blind to the power of 1 ... Q-B8!!

Double takes

In many a position a player takes for granted that a certain continuation is impossible. Or else he imagines that his opponent will have to defend against a certain threat.

Imagine that player's astonishment when the impossible turns out to be possible, and when his opponent lets him play a seemingly decisive move. In chess there's often more than meets the eye as in the following position. (*See Diagram 98*)

White does not care for the exchange of Queens, but if he plays 1 Q-B3, Black has 1 ... NxBP; 2 BxN, Q-R5ch followed by 3 ... QxB in reply.

Yet White plays:

Diagram 98 (*White to move*)

BLACK: Amateur

WHITE: Starr

      1 Q-B3!   . . .

On 1 . . . NxKP; 2 QxNP is a strong reply. So Black plays his little combination.

      1 . . .   NxBP?

      2 R-Q1!   . . .

An ugly surprise for Black. In order to keep . . . Q-R5ch in reserve, he must play the following awkward Queen move.

      2 . . .   Q-K2

Not . . . NxKP??? allowing white to win on the spot with 3 RxQch.

      3 N-Q5!   . . .

This leaves Black's Queen without a good move, as White attacks the Queen as well as the unhappy Knight, and keeps N-B7ch in reserve.

      3 . . .   N/B3xP

Praying for 4 NxQ?, NxQch; 5 PxN, NxB, etc.

      4 Q-N3!   . . .

Absolutely merciless. If now 4 . . . Q-Q1; 5 BxN, NxB; 6 N-B7ch wins Black's Queen. And 4 . . . Q-K3 will not do because of 5 N-B7ch.

      4 . . .   Q-Q3

5 BxN	NxB
6 N-B7ch	K-Q2
7 NxR!	Resigns

For White still wins the Black Queen anyway.

The following example from a 1956 team match between Germany and Austria is even more pointed.

Diagram 99 (*White to move*)

BLACK: Beni

WHITE: Dittmann

White's King Pawn needs protection. The simplest way to provide this protection is by 1 Q-K3. Instead, White coyly tries indirect protection.

1 KR-Q1?   . . .

The idea is that if 1 ... BxP?; 2 BxN, BxB; 3 NxB and White has won a piece.

And if 1 ... NxP?; 2 NxN, BxN; 3 BxB, KxB; 4 Q-Q4ch also wins a piece for White.

But Black has an unexpectedly powerful retort.

1 . . .   P-K4!!

If now 2 PxP, PxP; 3 BxP, QxQ; 4 RxQ, B-R3! and Black wins the Exchange.

Or if 2 PxP, PxP; 3 B-B5, QxQ; 4 RxQ, B-R3!; 5 BxR, BxR; 6 R-Q1, B-K6ch and Black wins a piece.

2 B-K3   NxP

Now this is safe, and leaves Black a Pawn ahead.

3 NxN   BxN

Black is unconcerned about 4 QxP, QxQ; 5 RxQ because of 5 . . . PxP!; 6 BxP, BxQNP, etc.

4 Q-N4   Q-K2!

Setting a new, delightful trap: 5 RxP, PxP; 6 BxP, B-Q5ch! (the Bishop is immune); 7 K-R1, QBxPch; 8 KxB, QxBch; 9 K-R3, Q-B6ch; 10 B-N3, B-B4 and wins.

5 P-B5   P-Q4

And Black wins easily with his advantage in position and material.

Wriggling out of trouble

To see such failures of imagination may be depressing, but imagination scores many triumphs too. These triumphs give us many of the most thrilling moments that a game of chess can provide. Take the magnificent play that develops from Diagram 100 as an outstanding example.

Diagram 100 (White to move)

BLACK

WHITE

Our first impression is that White is in a hopeless muddle, as his Knight is lost and his Rook is attacked.

Actually White has a very powerful asset—the opportunity to attack Black's exposed King.

1 R-K4ch   . . .

Salvaging his Rook. And note that 1 . . . KxP will not do because of 2 N-K5ch! winning the Queen.

This gives us the keynote to White's play: only forceful moves, such as checks, can possibly save him.

1 . . .   K-B1

This discreet withdrawal is compulsory, for after 1 . . . K-Q2 the simple reply 2 QxP leaves Black helpless against the threat of 3 P-B8/Q mate.

So White has another asset: the far-advanced passed Pawn. Which gives White a brilliant idea.

2 NxP!   . . .

With a view to 2 . . . QxQ; 3 R-K8ch, RxR; 4 PxR/Q mate!

2 . . .   QxN

Now White has seemingly shot his bolt.

3 R-K8ch!!   . . .

Interesting—but what good is it?

3 . . .   RxR

If . . . KxP; 4 RxR and White wins easily.

4 QxPch!!   . . .

The brilliant point.

4 . . .   KxQ

If 4 . . . K-K2; 5 P-B8/Q dbl ch is murderous.

5 PxR/Nch!   . . .

Delicious underpromotion.

5 . . .   K-B1

6 NxQ   . . .

With a Knight and three Pawns ahead, White wins the ending easily. Beautifully inventive play by White!

In the next position, from a tournament game played in Paris in 1931, Black's plight seems almost as desperate. True, his pieces are well placed, but he is *two* Exchanges down and his Queen is *en prise*.

The position seems to offer Black nothing, for example 1 ... Q-R4; 2 QR-B1, B-B3; 3 RxB!; PxR; 4 P-Q7 and White wins.

Black rightly concludes that only desperate measures can save him.

Diagram 101 (*Black to move*)

BLACK: Tjutsevich

WHITE: Crepeaux

Black's salvation measures are "in the air," so to speak, and yet it is not easy to see them. Somehow or other, we sense, Black should be able to make good use of that long diagonal against White's King:

<blockquote>1 ...   N-N6ch!!</blockquote>

Now White goes hopelessly wrong if he plays 2 PxN?? For then comes 2 ... B-B3ch; 3 K-R2, Q-R4 mate.

White can decline the Knight, to be sure, but after 2 K-N2, N-K7 dis ch Black wins White's Queen, with an easy victory in sight.

Hence White tries the most obvious reply.

<blockquote>2 QxN   B-B3ch</blockquote>

The move that Black wanted.

              3 K-N1   . . .

But now Black seemingly has only one check left—and he is hopelessly behind in material.

              3 . . .   Q-Q5ch
              4 Q-B2   . . .

There was more to Black's check than met the eye, for if 4 R-B2, QxQRch; 5 R-B1, Q-Q5ch forcing the draw!

              4 . . .   Q-KN5ch
              5 Q-N3   Q-Q5ch

Draw! White has no way of escaping from the devilish checks. A marvelously ingenious finish.

The situation in Diagram 102, which occurred in a game between two Rumanian players in 1955, is perhaps even more rewarding.

Diagram 102 (*White to move*)

BLACK: Gama

WHITE: Onesciuc

White's position seems to be in the last throes of desperation. True, he is a piece and a Pawn ahead, but what can he do in the face of Black's threat of . . . QxRPch and mate on the following move?

White's Queen is completely out of the battle, it would seem, and his other pieces are no great help either. Yet the stage is set for a magnificent defensive resource.

1 NxP!! . . .

This stops . . . QxRPch and also attacks Black's Queen.

If Black tries 1 . . . Q-N5 White has 2 N-Q2, Q-R6; 3 N-B1, N-B5; 4 QxKP! and suddenly White's Queen is back in play, preventing . . . Q-N7 mate—and Black's attack is repulsed.

1 . . . PxN

Why not?—and now the mating threat is on again. But with the King file open, White's pieces become ferociously active.

2 Q-N7ch!! . . .

A dazzling resource which saves White on the very brink of defeat.

2 . . . RxQ

Or 2 . . . KxQ; 3 PxQ, etc.

3 R-K8ch   R-N1
4 RxRch   KxR
5 PxQ   . . .

Thus the attack is beaten off, the Queens are gone, and White wins the endgame.

In Diagram 103 we have an enjoyably deceptive position. White is two pieces ahead, and ought to have an easy win. But Black is giving check, a move that must always be respected.

The more we look at the position of Diagram 103, the more desperate White's situation seems.

Thus, if 1 K-B1?, Q-B7 mate.

If 1 K-R1?, N-B7ch winning White's Queen.

If 1 K-N2?, Q-B7ch; 2 K-R3, QxRPch; 3 KxN, Q-R4 mate.

If 1 N-Q4?, RxN attacking White's Queen and threatening to win by a crushing double or discovered check.

Can it be that despite his overwhelming material advantage White is lost?

Diagram 103 (*White to move*)

BLACK: Dyner

WHITE: Oren

Luckily White has an amazing resource:

1 N-N6!!! . . .

This nonsensical-looking move wins for White! In fact, Black resigns on the spot, for if he plays 1 . . . RxN then 2 Q-Q4ch wins at once for White.

And if Black plays 1 . . . QxNch then White has 2 Q-Q4ch!! (the basic point of the defense), winning quite easily after 2 . . . RxQ; 3 RxQ—or 2 . . . QxQch; 3 NxQ, RxN; 4 BxN, etc.

A grand piece of alert defensive mastery.

Middle-game virtuosity

And so we come back to the point raised earlier in this book— that middle-game play is chess at its most thrilling. Particularly gripping are those middle-game struggles where both players are at their best, and where the issue is resolved only after a whole series of star moves.

What makes the play from Diagram 104 so interesting is that White has a chance to win a Pawn. But in order to do so he must jeopardize his whole positional advantage and run the risk of losing the game.

Most players would shrink from such a possibility. Yet in

chess there are times when a player cannot evade the issue and when he must accept the challenge, no matter how dangerous it looks.

Diagram 104 (*White to move*)

BLACK: Udovchich

WHITE: Bisguier

White sees that if he plays 1 RxP Black will reply 1 ... NxP so that if 2 QxN, RxB!; 3 RxR??, Q-K8 mate. Nevertheless White deliberately plays into this terrifying possibility.

> 1 RxP!   NxP!?
> 2 QxN   RxB!

(If 2 ... RxN?!; 3 R/B1-Q1!! wins for White!)

As we have seen, White must not play 3 RxR?? because of 3 ... Q-K8 mate.

In addition, White's Knight is threatened—or is it? White says no!

> 3 R/B1-Q1!   ...

White threatens 4 R-Q8ch, RxR; 5 RxR mate. Thus he has put his finger on a vulnerable spot in Black's game, and his Knight is safe, at least for the time being.

If now 3 ... R/B5-B1 (to guard the mating threat); 4 Q-Q2!, QxQ; 5 NxQ, R-Q1; 6 N-B1! and White maintains strong pressure.

<table>
<tr><td>3 . . .</td><td>P-B3</td></tr>
</table>

To relieve the mating threat.

<table>
<tr><td>4 R/Q6-Q3</td><td>. . .</td></tr>
</table>

Getting rid of the attack on his Knight.

<table>
<tr><td>4 . . .</td><td>Q-N4</td></tr>
<tr><td>5 R-Q8ch</td><td>RxR</td></tr>
<tr><td>6 RxRch</td><td>K-B2</td></tr>
<tr><td>7 RxB</td><td>. . .</td></tr>
</table>

So White has won a piece, but the game is far from over.

<table>
<tr><td>7 . . .</td><td>Q-K6</td></tr>
</table>

Threatening . . . Q-K8 mate.

(Note that Black does not threaten . . . QxN???, for after his Queen retakes he pins the Black Rook, preventing . . . R-B8ch followed by mate.)

<table>
<tr><td>8 P-R3</td><td>. . .</td></tr>
</table>

In the event of 8 Q-N1, Black regains the piece with . . . R-N5. But after White's last move, he is finally safe on the first rank, and need on longer fear a mating attack there.

<table>
<tr><td>8 . . .</td><td>R-N5</td></tr>
<tr><td>9 Q-Q2!</td><td>. . .</td></tr>
</table>

Forcing a winning endgame, for if 9 . . . QxN?; 10 Q-Q7ch, K-N3; 11 R-R7! is disastrous for Black.

<table>
<tr><td>9 . . .</td><td>RxN</td></tr>
</table>

Not 9 . . . QxQ?; 10 NxQ and White is a piece up.

<table>
<tr><td>10 QxQ</td><td>RxQ</td></tr>
<tr><td>11 R-R7ch</td><td>K-N3</td></tr>
<tr><td>12 RxRP</td><td>. . .</td></tr>
</table>

With a valuable Pawn to the good, White has a comfortable endgame win.

Thus White, by resourceful and imaginative play, has justified his initiative. This is a fine example of the role of creative imagination in chess. Technique is necessary and important, but from the point of view of how to enjoy chess, technique will always remain the handmaiden of imagination. For it will always be imagination that gives both the master and the *aficionado* their greatest pleasure in chess.

I think you will agree as you look back on this book as a whole that what we have been stressing all the time is the role of *imagination*. This applies to the composed endings, to the problems, to the master games. It is our imagination, after all, that is intrigued most by these delectable facets of chess. They take such a powerful hold on us that when we are preoccupied with chess, we forget about everything else—jobs, worries, sorrows, perhaps ill health.

As I wrote this book I felt that I was taking each reader on a grown-up voyage to Treasure Island—a voyage of discovery that will probably come as a complete revelation to him.

On this Treasure Island there is no competition, no pitchfork urging to improve, no exhortations to work hard. Instead, all my emphasis has been on the pleasure that chess offers us. My theme has truly been *how to enjoy chess*.

APPENDIX

Diagram 22. White can win if he can get his passed Rook Pawn rolling. But how? If 1 R-QN7, K-B7; 2 P-R7, R-R8 stops the Pawn. Or if 1 R-KB7, R-K8; 2 P-R7, R-K1.

The right way is:

> 1 R-KN7!   ...

If now 1 ... R-K8; 2 R-N1! (pinning!), RxR; 3 P-R7 and wins, as Black cannot play ... R-N1.

If 1 ... K-K7 or 1 ... K-Q7; 2 R-N2ch followed by 3 R-QR2 enforcing the queening of the Pawn, as Black cannot play ... R-R8.

> 1 ...   K-B7
> 2 R-N2ch   K-N6

If now 3 P-R7?, R-R8.

> 3 R-QR2!   ...

Threatening 4 P-R7, etc.

> 3 ...   KxR
> 4 P-R7 and wins

Black's King obstructs his Rook, so that 4 ... R-R8 is pointless.

Diagram 23. White is in a bad way, for Black's advanced Knight Pawn threatens to queen, and White seemingly cannot play 1 QxP/N2 because of 1 ... P-K7 dis ch followed by the queening of his King Pawn. Yet White goes into this desperate line, relying on no less than *three* distinct stalemates!

> 1 QxP/N2!!   P-K7 dis ch
> 2 K-N8   ...

Now it turns out that White need not fear 2 ... P-K8/Q, for in that case he has 3 Q-B3ch!, QxQ and White is stalemated! So Black tries another way:

> 2 ...   B-R7ch
> 3 K-B8!   ...

Now if 3 ... P-K8/Q; 4 Q-Q2ch!, QxQ and again White is stalemated! (Black's Bishops are too strong for his own good.)

> 3 ...   B-B4ch
> 4 K-Q8   P-K8/Q

A last attempt.

> 5 QxPch!   KxQ

And White is still stalemated!

Diagram 24. How White can possibly win in this barren-looking position is quite a puzzle. And yet it can be done. With the right kind of preliminary move, White can trap the Black Bishop!

1 P-B6!   . . .

Threatens 2 PxP followed by the queening of the Pawn.

Black cannot defend adequately with 1 ... P-N3 or 1 ... P-N4, for then White has 2 K-N7, B-Q1; 3 B-Q4, after which Black must lose his Bishop when White plays 4 K-B8.

1 . . .   PxP

Now the doom of Black's Bishop is sealed.

2 K-N7   B-Q1
3 K-B8   B-K2
4 K-Q7   B-B1

A thin sliver of hope: maybe the Black Bishop can escape to King Rook 3.

5 B-K3ch!   . . .

The composer has provided for every detail. Note how he placed the White King on a black square, subject to a check by White's Bishop to gain time and maintain the imprisonment of Black's Bishop.

5 . . .   K-B7
6 K-K8   B-N2
7 KxP   B-R1
8 K-N8 and wins

Journey's end. White has at last trapped the Bishop. After capturing the Bishop, he will win Black's Bishop Pawn and then advance and queen his own Knight Pawn.

Diagram 25. This study belongs in the category of compositions in which a Queen is demonstrated to be helpless.

Without being too systematic about it, we can observe the following about this position:

Black's King is wedged into the corner and may be subject to a mating attack. The presence of a White passed Queen Rook Pawn seems to indicate that White's attack will force the exchange of his Rook and Knight for Black's Queen, and then win by advancing and queening the Rook Pawn.

Therefore White's first move is fairly obvious:

1 R-K2   . . .

Threatens 2 R-K8ch, Q-N1; 2 RxQch, KxR; 3 P-R5 and the Pawn advances to queen. (Black's King cannot catch up with it.)

Black has little choice. If 1 ... K-N1??; 2 R-K8 mate.

If 1 ... P-R3; 2 R-K8ch, K-R2; 3 N-B6ch, K moves; 4 R-KN8ch winning the Black Queen.

Black's only defense is:

1 ...   Q-N1

This sets a cunning trap. After 2 N-B6 White attacks the Black Queen and also threatens R-K8. Black moves his Queen along the Knight file, say 2 ... Q-N8. Then if 3 R-K8ch, K-N2; 4 R-KN8ch, K-R3!!; 5 RxQ and Black is stalemated!

White avoids this devilish trap and finds a winning move even more diabolical:

2 N-N7!!   . . .

If now 2 ... QxN; 3 R-K8ch, Q-N1; 4 RxQch, KxR; 5 P-R5, etc., and White wins easily.

If 1 ... KxN; 2 R-KN2ch followed by 3 RxQch and 4 P-R5 winning in the same way.

Finally, if 1 ... P-R4; 2 R-K8, QxR; 3 NxQ, P-R5; 4 N-B6, P-R6; 5 N-N4 followed by the winning advance of White's Rook Pawn.

SOLUTIONS TO QUIZ ON CHESS PROBLEMS

Diagram 38. White has two batteries (Bishop and Knight and also Rook and Knight) trained on the Black King. Yet both rear men (the White Bishop and the White Rook) are under attack.

The surprising key move is 1 K-B2.

Black has no less than four checks, but none of them works.

If Black plays 1 . . . P-N6ch, White replies 2 NxP mate.

If Black plays 1 . . . R/N8-N7ch, his Bishop no longer attacks White's Rook. Consequently White replies 2 N/B1-K2 mate.

If Black plays 1 . . . R/N4-N7ch, his Rook no longer attacks White's Bishop. Consequently White replies 2 N/B3-K2 mate.

If Black plays 1 . . . B-B4ch, his Rook at Knight 4 no longer attacks White's Bishop. Consequently White replies 2 N-K4 mate.

If Black plays 1 . . . PxN, White replies 2 BxP mate.

On other Black moves, White replies 2 N-N3 mate (the threat after 1 K-B2).

Diagram 39. This is an easy problem with an attractive setting. The key move is 1 B-N5 with the threat of 2 B-R6 mate.

Black's only chance is to advance his King Pawn in order to create A flight square for his King.

However, after 1 . . . P-K3, Black's Queen no longer has access to Queen Bishop 1. Consequently White replies 2 Q-R8 mate.

And after 1 . . . P-K4, Black's Queen no longer has access to Queen Bishop 4. Consequently White replies 2 Q-R3 mate.

Diagram 40. This is puzzling at first sight, as Black's King threatens to play . . . K-N5 giving discovered check; he also threatens 1 . . . R-R8ch. The key move is 1 Q-R4, a magnificent waiting move which makes maximum use of the White Bishop's powers.

If Black plays 1 . . . K-N5 dis ch, White replies 2 BxR mate.

If Black plays 1 . . . RxN or 1 . . . QxN, White replies 2 B-N6 mate.

If Black plays 1 . . . Q-Q1 or 1 . . . Q-KB1, White replies 2 B-B6 mate.

If Black plays 1 . . . Q-R1, White replies 2 BxQ mate.

If Black plays 1 . . . P-B4, White replies 2 BxP mate.

If Black plays 1 ... P-K4, White replies 2 BxP mate.

If Black plays 1 ... R-KN8, White replies 2 BxR mate.

If Black plays 1 ... R-KB8, White replies 2 B-B2 mate.

If Black moves 1 ... R-K8, White plays 2 B-K3 mate.

If Black plays 1 ... R-QB8, White replies 2 B-B3 mate.

If Black plays 1 ... R-QN8, White replies 2 B-N2 mate.

If Black plays 1 ... R-R8ch, White replies 2 BxR mate.

On other moves, any discovered check with the White Bishop forces checkmate.

Diagram 41. This impressive problem illustrates the Novotny theme. (See the discussion of Diagram 27.) The key move is *1 N-Q7.* This threatens 2 Q-QB5 mate.

Black's dilemma is that if he plays ... BxN, his Rook at Queen Rook 2 is out of commission. If he plays ... RxN, his Bishop is useless.

Thus, if Black plays 1 ... BxN, White replies 2 B-K7 mate.

And if Black plays 1 ... RxN, White replies 2 R-N6 mate.

If Black plays 1 ... R-B3, White replies 2 QxB mate.

If Black plays 1 ... R-B2, White replies 2 Q-N6 mate.

If Black plays 1 ... B-N6ch, White replies 2 BxB mate.

If Black plays 1 ... B-N8, White replies 2 B-KN3 mate.

If Black plays any other move, White carries out his threat and replies 2 Q-QB5 mate.

BIBLIOGRAPHY

BIBLIOGRAPHY

IT HAS always been my stout conviction that chess is the most fascinating of all games. While others may disagree, there is one striking fact about the universal appeal of chess, and that is the huge literature it has inspired. It has been said that over 25,000 books have been written about the game.

To survey this field and choose the most worth-while items would be the task of highly competent specialists. What I propose to do here is to list some of the books from which I have derived the most pleasure and instruction. It is my hope that this listing will give you the same pleasure and instruction.

As this book stresses the pleasure to be obtained from great master games, I shall devote most of my attention to game collections. This type of reading matter is also the kind best calculated to raise your playing skill enormously. So, whether you wish to delve deeply or skim for your pleasure, this is the field that should interest you most.

For a start, let me recommend Irving Chernev's *1000 Best Short Games of Chess*. To my way of thinking, this book combines pleasure and instruction in what is really an ideal fashion. It starts with four-move games and progresses eventually to games of twenty-four moves —the maximum number. The games are fresh, piquant, concise. They make their point quickly and convincingly. They run the gamut of every conceivable kind of mistake and punishment. The book is a veritable encyclopedia of attacking motifs. Its entertaining character can be guessed by some of the leading themes: Quick Knockouts of Great Masters; Games Won by Celebrities; Games Won by Prodigies; Games won by Moving Pawns Only; Mate by Suffocation; Mate by Under-Promotion; The Deadly Quiet Move;

King Wanderings; Knight Gallopings; and the like. The notes are useful, often witty, and sometimes quietly mordant. As you will have guessed, this is a book of which I am very fond.

The finest all-round collection of a single player's games is undoubtedly Alexander Alekhine's *My Best Games of Chess* (two volumes, which may be obtained separately). For brilliancy and depth of strategy, these games are incomparable. The games sparkle with beautiful conceptions and striking surprise moves. No one who plays over these games will ever forget them, and they bear repeated study. In fact, their impact is heightened by repetition.

A companion volume, C. H. O'D. Alexander's *Alekhine's Best Games of Chess, 1938-1945,* is almost on the very same high level. It rounds out the career of this unique genius in a very satisfying way.

The Art of Sacrifice in Chess, by Rudolf Spielmann, is a great book on combinative play by a great master of the attack. It is a pedagogical book, but so illuminating in its insights and so rich in ideas that it will give you great pleasure. The games are among the choicest gems of attack that Spielmann produced in a lifetime of master play. The games stress the formation of a proper plan at the beginning of the middle game, and for this reason they are invaluable to the student.

In *The Immortal Games of Capablanca,* I have collected the best games of one of the great world champions. Capablanca played championship chess with an ease that baffled all his contemporaries. Just how he did it may be seen in these outstanding masterpieces. The attacks seem to play themselves, the endgames are marvels of deceptively simple technique. Capablanca was the great simplifier, and it is good for lesser players to see how much can be extracted from positions that might seem barren of possibilities.

Adventures of a Chess Master, by George Koltanowski, is a collection out of the ordinary. It contains the best blindfold games of a player who is universally acknowledged as one of the two best living practitioners of the art. There is also authoritative advice on how to play blindfold chess, a subject of perennial interest to all players. A colorful book and a colorful personality.

Another colorful personality, Frank Marshall, collected his best games in a book called *My Fifty Years of Chess.* Marshall was a born gambler, always ready to take a chance or call a bluff. He was the man who invented the term "swindle" for a trappy move that shouldn't work but probably will. There are 140 games, brimming with brilliant play, that make very enjoyable reading. The notes are first-class and contribute a great deal to the reader's pleasure.

A different approach to the game is seen in my book, *Tarrasch's Best Games of Chess*. Tarrasch was the great master of relentless system. (His game with Janowski, which starts on page 132 of this book, is a good example of his style.) Like an architect who starts with the plan of a building in his brain, Tarrasch built up massive structures long before their outlines were perceptible to the average player. This constructive feature is immensely valuable to the learner; it gives him a feeling for the conception and execution of long-range plans. Virtually every great player of the last seventy years has learned something from Tarrasch. Anyone who plays over these 183 games has made a mighty step forward in his understanding and appreciation of chess.

Morphy's Best Games of Chess, by P. W. Sergeant, is a delightful book by any standards and particularly rewarding to study at the same time as the Tarrasch book. Morphy is the master of quick development, the elegant attack, and the light touch. His opponents are crushed before they know what happened to them. These games, as someone has said, remind us of a Damascus blade cutting a silk cushion. The three hundred games in this volume make a rich feast of lighthearted play. This is a fine book to dip into and come back to repeatedly.

In *500 Master Games of Chess*, Tartakover and Du Mont have produced a book of very fine master games from every time and place and of every conceivable kind. These are choice games; they include the familiar, obligatory gems as well as much that is unfamiliar but very well worth knowing. The notes are not too detailed, but they are aphoristic and to the point.

Epic Battles of the Chessboard by R. N. Coles is a collection of great fighting games played by leading masters. Anyone who feels that chess does not require fighting qualities will be pleasantly surprised by this book. The games are heartily recommended to anyone who enjoys a good fight and likes to find excitement and suspense in his chess. Not the least delight afforded by these games is their seesaw quality, and as a rule the winner is the man who made the next to the last blunder. Each game is a Donnybrook Fair, and the admirable notes contribute greatly to the fun.

Chess Secrets by Edward Lasker is a book out of the ordinary. The author gives us his genial reminiscences of a lifetime of chess, and this should be particularly absorbing to anyone who wants to know what it is like to be a chessmaster. Into his account Lasker weaves the story of his acquaintance with many of the great players of his day. Interspersed throughout are many master games with excellent notes. This constant change of pace, from game to biography and then back again to another game, gives the book a very readable quality.

Fifty Great Games of Modern Chess, by H. Golombek, is an unpretentious and clearly written introduction to modern master play by a leading British player and journalist. This attractive little book makes a splendid introduction to some of the finest games produced since 1900.

My book, *Learn Chess From the Masters,* is devoted to a number of outstanding master games with a format that gives the reader a chance to guess the moves. The answers are graded, so that the reader has a chance to compare his score against the best possible score. This is a good way to study, as it supplies the spur of competition.

The Chess Mind, by Gerald Abrahams, is to my way of thinking one of the very best, and certainly one of the most original, books ever written on chess. Of making chess books there is no end, but few are as meaty and brilliantly written as this one. Such chapters as Vision in Chess; Common Sense and the Intrusion of Ideas; Imagination: Its Use and Abuse; How Battles are Won and Lost are unique in chess literature. One of the finest books ever written on chess.

Another book of mine, *The Great Chess Masters and Their Games,* is devoted to biographies of the world champions and some of their finest games. It is also a history of the development of chess theory from 1840 to our own time. The masters treated here are Adolf Anderssen: the Romantic; Paul Morphy: the Gentleman; Wilhelm Steinitz: the Lawgiver; Emanuel Lasker: the Philosopher; José Raoul Capablanca: the Machine; Alexander Alekhine: the Fighter; Max Euwe: the Logician.

In *1001 Brilliant Sacrifices and Combinations* I have provided 1001 diagrams in which a brilliant line of play wins for the player on the move. Solutions are given at the back of the book, so that the reader can work them out for himself. What Czerny and Moscheles have done for the aspiring pianist this book does for the chess student who wants to improve his play and enjoy himself in the process.

The Pleasures of Chess, by a man who calls himself "Assiac" (Caissa spelled backwards), is a very delightful book. It contains brilliant short games, amusing snippets, entrancing problems, and endgames, described in a witty and wryly humorous style. There are over forty positions for the reader to solve. This charmingly written book is a classic of its kind.

When we come to problems and endgames, the literature is sparse because some of the best books are out of print. This is unfortunately true of two outstanding works: Kenneth Howard's *How to Solve Chess Problems* and *The Enjoyment of Chess Problems*. These books are model works and can be unreservedly recommended.

The Macmillan Handbook of Chess contains satisfyingly long and expert chapters, with many fine examples, on problems and endgames. These chapters are written by P. L. Rothenberg, an outstanding authority in both fields. The definitions of technical terms and the classification of themes are particularly helpful.

Brian Harley's *Mate in Three Moves*, with 267 problems, is the classic work on this subject. Harley thoroughly dissects the anatomy of the three-move problem, and describes all its beautiful facets.

Chessboard Magic!, by Irving Chernev, makes an ideal introduction to the composed endgame. There are 160 masterpieces in this beautiful collection. The notes are written with an infectious zest that heightens the reader's pleasure.

Collection of Chess Studies, by A. A. Troitzky, contains 360 magnificent endgames by one of the titans of endgame composition. Unfortunately this gem-studded volume has been out of print for some time.

Tattersall's *1000 Endgames* is a monumental collection of superb endings. It was published about 1910 and has been out of print for a good many years.

However, the finest, most recent, and most inclusive work on endgame studies is *1234 Modern Endgame Studies*, by M. A. Sutherland and H. M. Lommer. Published in 1939, this book has been out of print for some years.

Among chess periodicals, there are two American and two English magazines of interest. *Chess Review* is in my opinion the best of the lot, with a well-rounded set of features. There is excellent coverage of chess events and a good Games Department ably annotated by Hans Kmoch. *Chess Caviar* is made up of attractive games of 20 moves or less. *Solitaire Chess* is devoted to a game with graded moves, so that the reader can grade his score. Past Masterpieces revives the glories of old-time master chess. Game of the Month is a current outstanding game annotated by a former world champion. Special articles, many diagrams and pictures, a long section for postal players, a choice collection of fine problems and endings round out each issue.

The American Chess Bulletin, which has been published since 1904, has a good games section and an excellent problem section. A drawback from the point of view of most readers is that no diagrams are used in the games.

The British Chess Magazine, now the oldest chess magazine in existence, goes back to 1882. However, it has kept abreast of the times, and has excellent departments devoted to annotated games, problems, and endgame studies, as well as special articles.

Chess, another English magazine of much more recent vintage, has good sections of annotated games and problems. It is edited in a lively fashion which sometimes verges on the sensational.

If you do not already subscribe to a magazine, you will find it worth-while to write for sample copies. In that way you can decide which magazine appeals best to you. A magazine is unquestionably the cheapest form of chess literature, and also the most varied and most interesting.

BOOKS

Irving Chernev: *The 1000 Best Short Games of Chess.* New York: Simon and Schuster.

Alexander Alekhine: *My Best Games of Chess, 1908–1923.* New York: Harcourt, Brace and Company. London: G. Bell & Sons.

Alexander Alekhine: *My Best Games of Chess, 1924–1937.* New York: Harcourt, Brace and Company. London: G. Bell & Sons.

C. H. O'D. Alexander: *Alekhine's Best Games of Chess, 1938-1945.* New York: Harcourt, Brace & Co. London: G. Bell & Sons.

Rudolf Spielmann: *The Art of Sacrifice in Chess.* New York: David McKay Company. London: G. Bell & Sons.

Fred Reinfeld: *The Immortal Games of Capablanca.* New York: Chess Review. London: Sir Isaac Pitman & Sons.

George Koltanowski: *Adventures of a Chess Master.* New York: David McKay Company.

Frank J. Marshall: *My Fifty Years of Chess*. New York: Chess Review. New York: David McKay Company. London: G. Bell & Sons.

Fred Reinfeld: *Tarrasch's Best Games of Chess*. New York: David McKay Company. London: Chatto and Windus.

P. W. Sergeant: *Morphy's Best Games of Chess*. New York: Dover Publications.

Dr. S. Tartakover and J. du Mont: *500 Master Games of Chess*. New York: David McKay Company. London: G. Bell & Sons.

R. N. Coles: *Epic Battles of the Chessboard*. New York: David McKay Company.

Edward Lasker: *Chess Secrets I Learned from the Masters*. New York: David McKay Company.

H. Golombek: *Fifty Great Games of Modern Chess*. David McKay Company. London: G. Bell & Sons.

Fred Reinfeld: *Learn Chess From the Masters*. New York: Dover Publications. (Also published under the title *Chess by Yourself*. London: Arco Publications.)

Gerald Abrahams: *The Chess Mind*. London: The English Universities Press.

Fred Reinfeld: *The Great Chess Masters and Their Games*. New York: Sterling Publishing Company. (Also published under the title *The Human Side of Chess*. London: Faber and Faber.)

Fred Reinfeld: *1001 Brilliant Chess Sacrifices and Combinations*. New York: Sterling Publishing Company. London: William Foulsham & Company.

Assiac: *The Pleasures of Chess*. New York: Simon and Schuster. London: Turnstile Press.

I. A. Horowitz and Fred Reinfeld: *The Macmillan Handbook of Chess*. New York: The Macmillan Company.

Brian Harley: *Mate in Three Moves*. New York: David McKay Company.

MAGAZINES

Chess Review, 250 West 57th Street, New York 19, N. Y.

The American Chess Bulletin, 150 Nassau Street, New York 38, N. Y.

British Chess Magazine, 20, Chestnut Road, West Norwood, London, S.E. 27.

Chess, Sutton Coldfield, England.

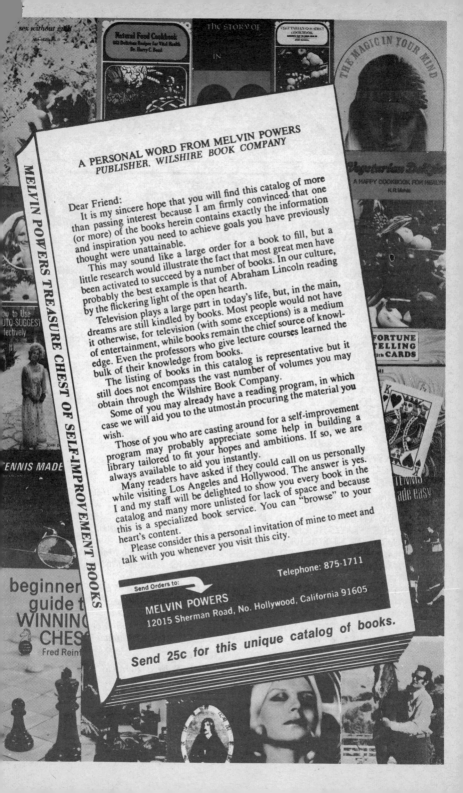

A PERSONAL WORD FROM MELVIN POWERS
PUBLISHER, WILSHIRE BOOK COMPANY

Dear Friend:

It is my sincere hope that you will find this catalog of more than passing interest because I am firmly convinced that one (or more) of the books herein contains exactly the information and inspiration you need to achieve goals you have previously thought were unattainable.

This may sound like a large order for a book to fill, but a little research would illustrate the fact that most great men have been activated to succeed by a number of books. In our culture, probably the best example is that of Abraham Lincoln reading by the flickering light of the open hearth.

Television plays a large part in today's life, but, in the main, dreams are still kindled by books. Most people would not have it otherwise, for television (with some exceptions) is a medium of entertainment, while books remain the chief source of knowledge. Even the professors who give lecture courses learned the bulk of their knowledge from books.

The listing of books in this catalog is representative but it still does not encompass the vast number of volumes you may obtain through the Wilshire Book Company.

Some of you may already have a reading program, in which case we will aid you to the utmost in procuring the material you wish.

Those of you who are casting around for a self-improvement program may probably appreciate some help in building a library tailored to fit your hopes and ambitions. If so, we are always available to aid you instantly.

Many readers have asked if they could call on us personally while visiting Los Angeles and Hollywood. The answer is yes. I and my staff will be delighted to show you every book in the catalog and many more unlisted for lack of space and because this is a specialized book service. You can "browse" to your heart's content.

Please consider this a personal invitation of mine to meet and talk with you whenever you visit this city.

Telephone: 875-1711

Send Orders to:

MELVIN POWERS
12015 Sherman Road, No. Hollywood, California 91605

Send 25c for this unique catalog of books.

Melvin Powers
SELF-IMPROVEMENT
LIBRARY

ASTROLOGY

ASTROLOGY: A FASCINATING HISTORY *P. Naylor*	2.00
ASTROLOGY: HOW TO CHART YOUR HOROSCOPE *Max Heindel*	2.00
ASTROLOGY: YOUR PERSONAL SUN-SIGN GUIDE *Beatrice Ryder*	2.00
ASTROLOGY FOR EVERYDAY LIVING *Janet Harris*	2.00
ASTROLOGY MADE EASY *Astarte*	2.00
ASTROLOGY MADE PRACTICAL *Alexandra Kayhle*	2.00
ASTROLOGY, ROMANCE, YOU AND THE STARS *Anthony Norvell*	3.00
MY WORLD OF ASTROLOGY *Sydney Omarr*	3.00
THOUGHT DIAL *Sydney Omarr*	2.00
ZODIAC REVEALED *Rupert Gleadow*	2.00

BRIDGE & POKER

ADVANCED POKER STRATEGY & WINNING PLAY *A. D. Livingston*	2.00
BRIDGE BIDDING MADE EASY *Edwin Kantar*	5.00
BRIDGE CONVENTIONS *Edwin Kantar*	4.00
COMPLETE DEFENSIVE BRIDGE PLAY *Edwin B. Kantar*	10.00
HOW TO IMPROVE YOUR BRIDGE *Alfred Sheinwold*	2.00
HOW TO WIN AT POKER *Terence Reese & Anthony T. Watkins*	2.00
SECRETS OF WINNING POKER *George S. Coffin*	3.00
TEST YOUR BRIDGE PLAY *Edwin B. Kantar*	3.00

BUSINESS STUDY & REFERENCE

CONVERSATION MADE EASY *Elliot Russell*	2.00
EXAM SECRET *Dennis B. Jackson*	2.00
FIX-IT BOOK *Arthur Symons*	2.00
HOW TO DEVELOP A BETTER SPEAKING VOICE *M. Hellier*	2.00
HOW TO MAKE A FORTUNE IN REAL ESTATE *Albert Winnikoff*	3.00
HOW TO MAKE MONEY IN REAL ESTATE *Stanley L. McMichael*	2.00
INCREASE YOUR LEARNING POWER *Geoffrey A. Dudley*	2.00
MAGIC OF NUMBERS *Robert Tocquet*	2.00
PRACTICAL GUIDE TO BETTER CONCENTRATION *Melvin Powers*	2.00
PRACTICAL GUIDE TO PUBLIC SPEAKING *Maurice Forley*	2.00
7 DAYS TO FASTER READING *William S. Schaill*	2.00
SONGWRITERS' RHYMING DICTIONARY *Jane Shaw Whitfield*	3.00
SPELLING MADE EASY *Lester D. Basch & Dr. Milton Finkelstein*	2.00
STUDENT'S GUIDE TO BETTER GRADES *J. A. Rickard*	2.00
TEST YOURSELF — Find Your Hidden Talent *Jack Shafer*	2.00
YOUR WILL & WHAT TO DO ABOUT IT *Attorney Samuel G. Kling*	2.00

CHESS & CHECKERS

BEGINNER'S GUIDE TO WINNING CHESS *Fred Reinfeld*	2.00
BETTER CHESS — How to Play *Fred Reinfeld*	2.00
CHECKERS MADE EASY *Tom Wiswell*	2.00
CHESS IN TEN EASY LESSONS *Larry Evans*	2.00
CHESS MADE EASY *Milton L. Hanauer*	2.00
CHESS MASTERY — A New Approach *Fred Reinfeld*	2.00
CHESS PROBLEMS FOR BEGINNERS *edited by Fred Reinfeld*	2.00
CHESS SECRETS REVEALED *Fred Reinfeld*	2.00

Melvin Powers
SELF-IMPROVEMENT
LIBRARY

CHESS STRATEGY — An Expert's Guide *Fred Reinfeld*	2.00
CHESS TACTICS FOR BEGINNERS *edited by Fred Reinfeld*	2.00
CHESS THEORY & PRACTICE *Morry & Mitchell*	2.00
HOW TO WIN AT CHECKERS *Fred Reinfeld*	2.00
1001 BRILLIANT WAYS TO CHECKMATE *Fred Reinfeld*	2.00
1001 WINNING CHESS SACRIFICES & COMBINATIONS *Fred Reinfeld*	3.00
SOVIET CHESS *Edited by R. G. Wade*	3.00

COOKERY & HERBS

CULPEPER'S HERBAL REMEDIES *Dr. Nicholas Culpeper*	2.00
FAST GOURMET COOKBOOK *Poppy Cannon*	2.50
HEALING POWER OF HERBS *May Bethel*	2.00
HERB HANDBOOK *Dawn MacLeod*	2.00
HERBS FOR COOKING AND HEALING *Dr. Donald Law*	2.00
HERBS FOR HEALTH How to Grow & Use Them *Louise Evans Doole*	2.00
HOME GARDEN COOKBOOK Delicious Natural Food Recipes *Ken Kraft*	3.00
MEDICAL HERBALIST *edited by Dr. J. R. Yemm*	3.00
NATURAL FOOD COOKBOOK *Dr. Harry C. Bond*	2.00
NATURE'S MEDICINES *Richard Lucas*	2.00
VEGETABLE GARDENING FOR BEGINNERS *Hugh Wiberg*	2.00
VEGETABLES FOR TODAY'S GARDENS *R. Milton Carleton*	2.00
VEGETARIAN COOKERY *Janet Walker*	2.00
VEGETARIAN COOKING MADE EASY & DELECTABLE *Veronica Vezza*	2.00
VEGETARIAN DELIGHTS — A Happy Cookbook for Health *K. R. Mehta*	2.00
VEGETARIAN GOURMET COOKBOOK *Joyce McKinnel*	2.00

HEALTH

DR. LINDNER'S SPECIAL WEIGHT CONTROL METHOD	1.00
GAYELORD HAUSER'S NEW GUIDE TO INTELLIGENT REDUCING	3.00
HELP YOURSELF TO BETTER SIGHT *Margaret Darst Corbett*	2.00
HOW TO IMPROVE YOUR VISION *Dr. Robert A. Kraskin*	2.00
HOW YOU CAN STOP SMOKING PERMANENTLY *Ernest Caldwell*	2.00
LSD — THE AGE OF MIND *Bernard Roseman*	2.00
MIND OVER PLATTER *Peter G. Lindner, M.D.*	2.00
NEW CARBOHYDRATE DIET COUNTER *Patti Lopez-Pereira*	1.00
PSYCHEDELIC ECSTASY *William Marshall & Gilbert W. Taylor*	2.00
YOU CAN LEARN TO RELAX *Dr. Samuel Gutwirth*	2.00
YOUR ALLERGY—What To Do About It *Allan Knight, M.D.*	2.00

HOBBIES

BLACKSTONE'S MODERN CARD TRICKS *Harry Blackstone*	2.00
BLACKSTONE'S SECRETS OF MAGIC *Harry Blackstone*	2.00
COIN COLLECTING FOR BEGINNERS *Burton Hobson & Fred Reinfeld*	2.00
400 FASCINATING MAGIC TRICKS YOU CAN DO *Howard Thurston*	3.00
GOULD'S GOLD & SILVER GUIDE TO COINS *Maurice Gould*	2.00
HOW I TURN JUNK INTO FUN AND PROFIT *Sari*	3.00
HOW TO WRITE A HIT SONG & SELL IT *Tommy Boyce*	7.00
JUGGLING MADE EASY *Rudolf Dittrich*	2.00
MAGIC MADE EASY *Byron Wels*	2.00

_____SEXUALLY ADEQUATE FEMALE *Frank S. Caprio, M.D.*   2.00
_____SEXUALLY ADEQUATE MALE *Frank S. Caprio, M.D.*   2.00
_____YOUR FIRST YEAR OF MARRIAGE *Dr. Tom McGinnis*   2.00

METAPHYSICS & OCCULT

_____BOOK OF TALISMANS, AMULETS & ZODIACAL GEMS *William Pavitt*   3.00
_____CONCENTRATION—A Guide to Mental Mastery *Mouni Sadhu*   3.00
_____DREAMS & OMENS REVEALED *Fred Gettings*   2.00
_____EXTRASENSORY PERCEPTION *Simeon Edmunds*   2.00
_____FORTUNE TELLING WITH CARDS *P. Foli*   2.00
_____HANDWRITING ANALYSIS MADE EASY *John Marley*   2.00
_____HANDWRITING TELLS *Nadya Olyanova*   3.00
_____HOW TO UNDERSTAND YOUR DREAMS *Geoffrey A. Dudley*   2.00
_____ILLUSTRATED YOGA *William Zorn*   2.00
_____IN DAYS OF GREAT PEACE *Mouni Sadhu*   2.00
_____KING SOLOMON'S TEMPLE IN THE MASONIC TRADITION *Alex Horne* 5.00
_____MAGICIAN — His training and work *W. E. Butler*   2.00
_____MEDITATION *Mouni Sadhu*   3.00
_____MODERN NUMEROLOGY *Morris C. Goodman*   2.00
_____NUMEROLOGY—ITS FACTS AND SECRETS *Ariel Yvon Taylor*   2.00
_____PALMISTRY MADE EASY *Fred Gettings*   2.00
_____PALMISTRY MADE PRACTICAL *Elizabeth Daniels Squire*   3.00
_____PALMISTRY SECRETS REVEALED *Henry Frith*   2.00
_____PRACTICAL YOGA *Ernest Wood*   3.00
_____PROPHECY IN OUR TIME *Martin Ebon*   2.50
_____PSYCHOLOGY OF HANDWRITING *Nadya Olyanova*   2.00
_____SEEING INTO THE FUTURE *Harvey Day*   2.00
_____SUPERSTITION — Are you superstitious? *Eric Maple*   2.00
_____TAROT *Mouni Sadhu*   4.00
_____TAROT OF THE BOHEMIANS *Papus*   3.00
_____TEST YOUR ESP *Martin Ebon*   2.00
_____WAYS TO SELF-REALIZATION *Mouni Sadhu*   2.00
_____WITCHCRAFT, MAGIC & OCCULTISM—A Fascinating History *W. B. Crow* 3.00
_____WITCHCRAFT — THE SIXTH SENSE *Justine Glass*   2.00
_____WORLD OF PSYCHIC RESEARCH *Hereward Carrington*   2.00
_____YOU CAN ANALYZE HANDWRITING *Robert Holder*   2.00

SELF-HELP & INSPIRATIONAL

_____CYBERNETICS WITHIN US *Y. Saparina*   3.00
_____DAILY POWER FOR JOYFUL LIVING *Dr. Donald Curtis*   2.00
_____DOCTOR PSYCHO-CYBERNETICS *Maxwell Maltz, M.D.*   3.00
_____DYNAMIC THINKING *Melvin Powers*   1.00
_____GREATEST POWER IN THE UNIVERSE *U. S. Andersen*   4.00
_____GROW RICH WHILE YOU SLEEP *Ben Sweetland*   2.00
_____GROWTH THROUGH REASON *Albert Ellis, Ph.D.*   3.00
_____GUIDE TO DEVELOPING YOUR POTENTIAL *Herbert A. Otto, Ph.D.*   3.00
_____GUIDE TO LIVING IN BALANCE *Frank S. Caprio, M.D.*   2.00
_____GUIDE TO RATIONAL LIVING *Albert Ellis, Ph.D. & R. Harper, Ph.D.*   3.00
_____HELPING YOURSELF WITH APPLIED PSYCHOLOGY *R. Henderson*   2.00
_____HELPING YOURSELF WITH PSYCHIATRY *Frank S. Caprio, M.D.*   2.00
_____HOW TO ATTRACT GOOD LUCK *A. H. Z. Carr*   2.00
_____HOW TO CONTROL YOUR DESTINY *Norvell*   2.00
_____HOW TO DEVELOP A WINNING PERSONALITY *Martin Panzer*   3.00
_____HOW TO DEVELOP AN EXCEPTIONAL MEMORY *Young & Gibson*   3.00
_____HOW TO OVERCOME YOUR FEARS *M. P. Leahy, M.D.*   2.00
_____HOW YOU CAN HAVE CONFIDENCE AND POWER *Les Giblin*   2.00
_____HUMAN PROBLEMS & HOW TO SOLVE THEM *Dr. Donald Curtis*   2.00
_____I CAN *Ben Sweetland*   3.00
_____I WILL *Ben Sweetland*   2.00
_____LEFT-HANDED PEOPLE *Michael Barsley*   3.00
_____MAGIC IN YOUR MIND *U. S. Andersen*   3.00
_____MAGIC OF THINKING BIG *Dr. David J. Schwartz*   2.00

*The books listed above can be obtained from your book dealer or directly from
Melvin Powers. When ordering, please remit 25c per book postage & handling.
Send 25c for our illustrated catalog of self-improvement books.*

Melvin Powers

12015 Sherman Road, No. Hollywood, California 91605

WILSHIRE HORSE LOVERS' LIBRARY

Notes

Notes